WHY ISLAM FORBIDS INTOXICANTS AND GAMBLING

WHY ISLAM

FORBIDS

INTOXICANTS AND GAMBLING

By

Muhammad Iqbal Siddiqi

A CENTRE OF ISLAMIC BOOKS

IDARA ISHA'AT-E-DINIYAT (P) LTD.

168/2, Jha House, Hazrat Nizamuddin
New Delhi-110 013 (India)

ISBN 81-7101-221-3

Why Islam Forbids Intoxicants and Gambling

by
Muhammad Iqbal Siddiqi

First Edition 1997

Published by
IDARA ISHA'AT-E-DINIYAT (P) LTD.
168/2, Jha House, Hazrat Nizamuddin
New Delhi-110013, (India)
Tel. Office : 692-6832, 692-6833
Tel. Showroom :463-1786, 461-6786
Fax : +91-11-693-2787 & 463-2786
E_mail : IDARA@giasdl 01.vsnl.net.in

Typesetting by:
DM Computer Designer & Composer
Delhi Cantt-110010, Tel. : 3293825

Printed at
Johar Offset Printers, Maujpur, Delhi

بِسْمِ اللّٰهِ الرَّحْمٰنِ الرَّحِيْمِ○

In the name of Allah, the Beneficent, the Merciful

يَا أَيُّهَا الَّذِيْنَ امَنُوْا إِنَّمَا الْخَمْرُ وَ الْمَيْسِرُ وَ الْأَنْصَابُ
وَ الْأَزْلَامُ رِجْسٌ مِّنْ عَمَلِ الشَّيْطَانِ فَاجْتَنِبُوْهُ لَعَلَّكُمْ
تُفْلِحُوْنَ○

"O Believers! surely wine and games of chance, (ungodly) shrines, and divining devices, are an abomination of Satan's work. Avoid them, that ye may prosper.

(5:90)

Contents

Page

Preface

CHAPTER 1

Teaching of Various Religions on Wine-Drinking

Hinduism 1
Zoroastrianism 3
Israelite religion 4
People of the Gospel and Prohibition of Wine 5
Use of Alcohol by the Ancient Arabs 6
Prohibition of Alcoholic Intoxicants is an Achievement of Islam 8

CHAPTER 2

Alcoholism

What does Alcohol do? 12
Basic material used in the preparation of Wine 13
How are Alcoholic Beverages made? 14
Some Important Kinds of Wine 15
What part did Alcohol Play in the Primitive Life? 16

CHAPTER 3

Al-Khamr

Meaning of Al-Khamr 18
Definition of Al-Khamr according to the Islamic Shari'ah 18
Al-*Khamr*..... Its Names and Attributes 19
Abstinents in the Pre-Islamic Arabia 22
Traditions on the Prohibition of Al-Khamr 23

Page

(a) Every Intoxicant is Unlawful 24
(b) Intoxicant even in Smallest Quantity is Unlawful 27
(c) A Drunkard is not a Believer 29
(d) A Habitual Drunkard will not Enter Paradise 29
(e) The Cursed Ten Persons 30
(f) Wine is a Disease 30
(g) Wine should not be offered as a Gift 30
(h) No Excuse for Wine-Drinking 31
(i) A Drunkard is a Worshipper of Idol 31

Prohibition of Wine in Islam — Brief History 31
The Background to Revelation of Verses on the Unlawfulness of Wine 33
Gradual Prohibition of *Khamr* in Islam 34
Immediate Submission of the Companions to the Commandment Declaring Wine Unlawful 43
Wine is no Cure for diseases but an Ailment 45
Is Wine an Impurity? 47
Rent of Building and Wages of Worker Engaged for Extracting Wine are Unlawful 48
Some Strange Stories about Drunkards 49

CHAPTER 4

The True Motive in the Prohibition of Khamr 53

CHAPTER 5

Evil Effects of Drinking Wine and other Intoxicant 59

Temporal

(a) Intellectual 59

Page

(b) Physical 60
(c) Economic 64
(d) Psychological Harms 65
(e) Social Harms 65
Spiritual 66
Paltry Benefits of Wine 69

CHAPTER 6

Some Expert opinion about Alcohol and Modern Researches on Alcoholism 71
Some Expert opinion about Alcohol 71
Modern Researches on Alcohol and its Action on the Human Organism 73

CHAPTER 7

Smoking is also Injurious to Health 81

CHAPTER 8

The Alcoholic's Problems 84
The Role of Alcohol in Sexual Relationship 84
The Alcoholic's Family Problems 85

CHAPTER 9

The Islamic Law and the Alcoholics 87
Punishment 87
Pre-requisites of Punishment 89
Mode of Evidence 91
Mode of Execution 95

Page

CHAPTER 10

Al-Maisir (Gambling) 97

Definition 97

The Holy Qur'an on the Prohibition of Gambling 98

Traditions on the Prohibition of Gambling 99

Stone-alters 100

Scriptures on the Unlawfulness of Gambling 101

A Brief History of the Prohibition of Gambling in Islam 101

Nature of Gambling and the Arabs 102

Divining Arrows Seeking Fortune 102

Difference Between Lots and Game of Chance 104

CHAPTER 11

Evil Effects of Gambling 107

Evil Effects 107

Paltry Benefits of Gambling 108

CHAPTER 12

Emphasis on the Unlawfulness of Wine and Gambling 111

CHAPTER 13

Conclusion

Gleanings from the Holy Qur'an 115

Bibliography 117

Index 119

Preface

At the present time, there is world oncern about increasing alcohol use and gambling. Most of the countries are therefore, facing growing problems arising from these diabolic acts.

The intoxicating liquor and gambling are the most vicious curses to humanity. They have ruined innumerable lives, shattered multitudes of homes, and caused more misery to mankind than all other vices put together. The civilized countries have failed to ban the brewing, purveying and consumption of intoxicants because the traffic in alcoholic liquor brings them huge revenues which they dislike losing.

Wine-drinking is a serious crime. A drunkard in intoxication is deprived of making distinction between right and wrong, virtue and vice, good and evil. His actions result into enmity and hatred which disturb the peace and tranquility of the society. Gambling is also a sin which destroys our wealth. These moral vices are injurious to the healthy atmosphere of the society.

Islam stands unique among all religions and among all systems, in the prohibition of wine and gambling and in basing that prohibition on reason. This book offers a study of the successful movement of Islam in its endeavour to eradicate the evils of wine-drinking and gambling.

This book is not intended to be the last word on the subject. It is, however, hoped that the people who sincerely want to understand the subject will find enough material in it for their satisfaction.

In the end, I must express my gratitude to my younger brother Mr. Muhammad Ikram Siddiqi for making useful suggestions regarding this book.

Mohammad Iqbal Siddiqi

CHAPTER 1

Teaching of Various Religions on Wine-Drinking

In order to elucidate the value of Islamic teachings about the prohibition of intoxication liquors, we shall first give the teaching of other religions on this subject. We begin with the religion which claims to be the oldest *viz.*,the Vedic religion.

Hinduism

It requires no deep research to know the teaching of the Hindu religion on wine-drinking. The religion is founded on the Vedas which throw more then sufficient light on this subject. From the Vedas, particularly the Rig Veda which is the most important of the four Vedas, it appears that the use of wine is not only allowed in the Hindu religion but also on certain occasions its use is both essential and meritorious. The ancient *rishis*, far from having any loathing for wine, regarded it as pure and sacred—something which added to one's sanctity and served as a means of bringing one nearer to the Holy souls. Vedic *Mantras* display before our eyes a panorama of the solemn effort which to win the pleasure of the *Parmatma* by making an offering of wine, and we find that in the sacred ritual of an Indian worshipper wine plays a greater part than all other things. He not only himself partakes of the juice of the *soma*, but washes therewith many of the articles which he uses in his worship and makes an offering of it to Indra and other gods for securing their favour.

Similarly, from the *mantras* which have been prescribed in the *Atharva Veda* for recitation on the occasion of the worship of the Ashuni Kumar gods it appears that the worshipper of ancient India believed wine to be such a blessed thing that he not only partook of it himself but begged his gods to do the same. In the *Atharva Veda, Kand* 9, *Adhiyai* 1, *Mantra* 17, we have the following prayer:

> "O Rishi Kumars! May the *madh* (wine) which is found in the mountains and wild herbs and plants and which is secreted on the occasion of *yaggiah*-may the sap thereof be for me and for you!"

In the above *mantras*, the god is not only requested to partake of wine, but at the time of worship of the crystal-made *yantar*, the devotee goes a step further: the god is bathed in wine, as if he is actually made to partake of wine. This ceremony is accompanied by a recitation of the following Vedic *Mantra*:

> "O crystal-made *yantar*! stay in our house as our guest. We offer to you *ghi*, wine, honey and sweet eatables of a similar kind. Always think of what is good for us, just as a father thinks of such things as are good for his children."[1]

The above two *mantras* show that the devotees of ancient India begged their gods to partake of wine, that they partook of it themselves and dipped therein the crystal-made *yantar*. But from *Kand* 10, *Adhiyai* 10, *Mantra* 10 of the same Veda it further appears that the gods themselves indulged in wine-drinking while celebrating their victories. The *mantra* runs thus:

> "Indra drank cups of wine, to get a victory by vanquishing his foe"

In the present age, some members of the Aryamat, while explaining the words *Soma* and such other words, have tried to show that the Vedas make no mention of wine, but that by the juice of *Soma* is meant the sap of wall-wort. But when we look at the practice of the whole Hindu nation on the one hand, and take into consideration, on

1. *Atharua Veda, Kand* 10, *Adhiyai* 6, *Mantras* 26 and 27.

the other, the fact that they have never had occasion to mix freely and for a long time, with any people that were given to wine-drinking which may lead us to conclude that they contacted these habits from other people, we cannot but hesitate to accept such explanations. Nay, when we read *Atharva Veda*, *Kand* 18, *Anuvak* 1, *Sukat* 1, *Mantra* 48, it becomes impossible for us to take such interpretations as true; for therein we find the following description of *Soma*:

> "This *Soma* is very flavoury and palatable, partly sweet and partly acid and sour. No enemy can stand against the god of Indra who partakes of such a *Soma*."

All the foregoing quotations go to prove that the Hindu religion gives full sanction for the use of wine and holds it to be indispensable for certain religious services. This conclusion is supported by Hindu usage and is confirmed by history.

In giving these quotations here it is not our object to criticize the Hindu religion or the *Vedas*. Our only object is to show that the Hindu religion does not forbid wine, rather it permits and even approves of its use.

Zoroastrianism

Another ancient religion is the Iranian religion. The Iranian people have a long continuous history and recent research shows that their civilization might be older than even the Vedic civilization. Both the ancient and the modern religions of these people show that wine was permitted.

Students of Zoroastrianism know that Zoroaster was not the founder of any new religion but that he only revived the ancient Iranian religion which had become corrupt owing to lapse of time. Hence in order to know the teaching of the Iranian religion about wine we must look at both the pre-Zoroastrian and the post-Zoroastrian periods.

Though from history it appears that the Iranians freely indulged in wine-drinking, yet how they regarded it from the religious point of view can be seen only from the Zoroastrian literature. The *Pahlavi* books, while discribing the nativity of Zoroastrian state that an angel handed a cup of wine to Zoroaster's farther Pourushasapa who drank it. Soon after his wife Daghdo conceived and gave birth to a child who was destined to usher in a new era in the history of the East.

The fact that as a preparatory to the birth of a Holy man, an angel gave a cup of wine to that Holy man's father to drink shows that even before the time of Zoroaster drinking wine was not only permissible but even meritorious.

Even the Iranian religion as reformed by Zoroaster holds drinking wine to be a meritorious act; for wine has an important part to play in the ceremonies performed at a time when Afringan's'prayers, which are designed specially for recital by Zoroastrian priests, are offered. At the time of the recital of these prayers, the Dastur seats himself on a carpet spread on the ground and has in front of him, in a metal plate or on the leaf of a tree, the best fruits and the choicest flowers of the season and has also before him vessels full of fresh milk and wine and also vessels containing fresh water and some refreshing sweet beverages.

In short, even according to the Iranian religion, the use of wine is recognized as commendable and praiseworthy and at the performance of certain religious ceremonies it is held to be essential to use it or have it nearby.

Israelite religion

The other ancient religion which comes next is the Israelite religion. This religion, too, like Hinduism and Zoroastrianism, is believed to trace its origin to the beginning of creation. The history of this religion, too, shows that the practice of drinking wine is as old as the world itself.

People of the Gospel and Prohibition of wine

We find in the *Torah*:

> "The Lord interculated with Aaron (Harun) saying: "Drink not wine and any intoxicant, you and your descendants, that you may not ruin: (it is) an obligation upon your descendants for ever."

In the Book of Maxims of the Prophet Solomon (Sulaiman) we read:

> "For whom is ruin? For whom is wretchedness? For whom lies contentions? For whom is distress? For whom are wounds without any cause and whose eyes are contracted? For those who are addicted to wine — those who are in quest for a bitter mixture of wine."
>
> "Look not towards wine when it turns red as it bubbles in the goblet and becomes very light to give pleasant taste."
>
> "But in the long run it stings the skin like a serpent and a snake."
>
> *(Chapter 23, Verses: 29-33)*
>
> "Be not among the drunkards, among those who ruin their bodies, for the drunkards and extravagants create dissensions; and those who sleep wear rags."
>
> *(Chapter 23, Verses: 20,21)*
>
> "Wine makes man a laughing stock and a drunkard turns himself vociferous and whosoever reels with both of them is not a wise-man."
>
> *(Chapter 20, Verses: 1, 2)*

In the Book of Ushah (peace be upon him), we read:

> "Fornication and wine and juice of grapes injure the heart."
>
> *(Chapter 4, Verse 11)*

In the Book of Prophet Sha'ya we find:

> "Ruin is for those who vax proud in the morning, follow the drunkards and lag behind in Divine blessings whereof wine makes them forgetful."
>
> *(Chapter 5, Verse: 11)*

"Eat not all that come out of wine stock and drink not wine or an intoxicant; and eat not all impure things."

(Book of Judges, Chapter 13, Verse: 14)

In the Book of Prophet Armaya (peace be upon him), we have:

"Drink not wine, you and your descendants, to the eternity."

(Chapter 35, Verse 6)

Verse 3 of Chapter 4 of the Book of Peter I reads as:

"Indeed we know the people who indulged in wickedness and ambitions as well as in addiction to wine, pride and group drinking and the unlawful worship of idols."

In the letter of Bolis addressed to the people of Afsus, we find:

"And be not drunkard with wine wherein lies debauchee but be filled with spirit."

From the above quotations we can derive that ruin, wretchedness, excitement of indignation, distress, bloody wounds, soring of eyes, trials and destructions, sting of the serpents, ruin of health, tomfoolery, mockery, scoff, debauchee, confusion, loss of intellect, heart-failure—all these abominable things victimize a person who drinks wine that is unlawful like ingratitude of Divine grace, arrogance and worship of idols.

Use of Alcohol by the Ancient Arab

Drinking wine was deeply rooted in the nature of the Arab before the dawn of Islam. No house was free from it and majority of the people was addicted to it. The Arab women prepared it and men praised it in their poetry. They considered it advantageous because they extracted huge profits by dealing in wine.

The history of the pre-Islamic Arab world reveals that alcoholic drinks had become indispensable for the life of the Arabs. Heavy drinking and the generous serving of alcoholic drinks were the signs of magnanimity for which the individual and the tribe received great honours and praise. Ancient Arab poetry and other literature is replete with praises of drinking wine and gambling as signs of manhood and chauvinism. Alyashkari, an ancient Arab poet says:

> When I am drunk I am the Lord
> Of Persian palaces of marvel;
> When I wake up, I am the Lord
> Of my little goat and camel.
> I love her (the goat) and she loves me.
> So camel loves her, she too loves. [2]

In fact the sale of wine was so customary that the Arabic word *tajir* which literally means merchant, had become synonym for the wine-sellers. The shops and bars of these wine-merchants remained open throughout the day and the night and were clearly designated with special flags. Thus the Arabs developed a rich taste for different kinds of locally extracted and imported alcoholic drinks. They formulated hundreds of words to describe different types of wine regarding their origin, the degrees of their alcohol concentration, the fruits from which they were extracted, the way they were fermented, their effect on the drunkard, the degree of their purity, their colour, their taste, and many more qualities. [3]

The Arabs had also perceived natural insight into the psychic effects of alcohol intake and the individual differences between people in this respect. For example, Al-Nuwairi refers to an old man to whom some friends complained about the excessive drinking of his three sons. "Describe them to me when they are drunk," said the old man. They answered, "When drunk the first one becomes very aggressive. He attacks his friends and tears their clothes. The second vomits making his clothes dirty. As for the third one, he is the best.

2. Al-Nuwairi, op. cit., Vol. IV, P. 104.
3. Al-Nuwairi, op. cit., IV. p. 86.

He becomes extremely quiet and polite." The old man's comments were, "the first and second will eventually become dry, but the third will never stop drinking ! "[4]

So it was only natural for the men who grew up in this alcohol saturated environment, and who were brought up in such a romantic society which placed great competitive emphasis on price, with such deep seated feelings of insecurity, of real and imagined dangers, to seek this pride with security in the fantasy of alcoholic intoxication.

From the quotations given above, it appears that from the beginning of the world to the time of the Holy Prophet (peace and blessings of Allah be upon him) wine-drinking was not declared as unlawful. On the other hand wine was even held as an essential part of some of the religious ceremonies and it was regarded as an hallowed and beneficial thing.

It was left to Islam, and Islam alone, to condemn this curse in unequivocal terms and ban its production, sale and consumption.

Prohibition of Alcoholic Intoxicants is an Achievement of Islam

When the order for the prohibition of *Khamr* (intoxicants) was promulgated by Islam, all other religions of the world instead of forbidding wine favoured its use, and in some of them it formed an indispensable part of certain sacred ceremonies. Under such circumstances, it was not an ordinary thing for Islam to prohibit wine. The world was not yet prepared to recognise the value of this Commandment. The medical authorities of the age held wine to be an excellent and highly invigorating beverage and they prescribed its use. They believed it to be extremely beneficial to health. But in spite of all these things Islam forbade wine and totally prohibited its use.

4. Ibid., p. 104.

The prohibition, too, was not given in an arbitrary way, but was supported by candid arguments. The arguments, too, are not biased, and its prohibition is accompanied by the admission that it has certain benefits.

Some philosophers may have, under certain circumstances, looked upon the use of wine with disfavour but no other system has solved this question in the way in which Islam has done it. Jainism, for instance, which is, truly speaking, not a religious system, but a philosophy, does, in a way, prohibit wine, but the question is, on what ground does it prohibit it? The prohibition is not based on reason or any medical ground and no argument has been given to show that wine is in any way injurious. The only reason for which Jainism forbids wine is that its preparation involves the destruction of life and as according to Jaini principles, it is unlawful to destory life, therefore it is held to be improper for the perfect followers of Jainism to drink wine.

Thus it is clear that Jainism does not promulgate a general prohibition of wine nor does it base its prohibition on the fact that wine, in itself, is an injurious thing and that the drinking thereof will produce an evil effect on those who consume it. The only reason for which Jainism disapproves of the use of wine is that its preparation involves a violation of the fundamental principle of Jainism which holds it to be unlawful to destroy life under any circumstances.

It short, Islam stands unique among all religions and among all systems, in the prohibition of wine and in basing that prohibition on reason. And what further compels our admiration for Islam is the fact that the Commandment was given at a time when the people were not prepared to fully understand its significance.

Some Muslims may take the attitude of those historians who have a vested interest in the uniqueness of events and situations and propose that the whole story of the success of the prohibition of

Khamr in *Madinah* was simply a miraculous achievement of Islam, of its blessed Prophet and of its Holy Book. An approach of analytical social science, on the other hand, may require more convincing arguments that this was so. This latter approach may on the contrary bring out a number of interesting generalizations and hypothesis.

Modern social scientists believe that there is no singular theory of social change; some assert that it may be a waste of time to look for such global explanations of social change. They all accordingly agree that the layman's attitude of pointing to a single isolated factor as the only cause of major social change is nothing more than a mythical contention. Human collective behaviour is too complex for behavioural scientists to observe single isolated cause followed by single isolated effect. This is so because the causes themselves have causes and their effects have other effects that may in turn become causes for other effects in the intricate network of social cobweb.

With this modern outlook to social change, are we justified in asserting that Islam is the only or even the major single cause for the revolutionary success of anti-alcohol dependence campaign in Madinah? Without any religious bias the answer is "yes, it is." It is at least the single major cause. This proposition is not a layman's attitude nor does it conflict with the pluralistic approach of modern social science.

When we speak of the influence of Islam in bringing about major revolutionary changes in the life of the pre-Islamic Arabs, are we referring to its greatest contribution of transforming primitive ignorants from the crude concreteness of prostrating themselves to stone gods which they had carved with their own hands to the most pure and abstract belief of monotheism of "there is no god but Allah", the Almighty, the Lord of the earth and the heavens?" Are we talking about the cardinal inspiration of Prophet Muhammad's life which was a human testimony of the Revelation he received and who was loved and revered as no other man was? Are we thinking of the considerable inspiration of collective and individual Islamic rituals of prayer, Fasting and Zakat in the life of pioneer Muslims? Are we referring to the Holy Qur'an, its style of stirring eloquence which defied the Arabs with its monumental beauty and which remains to this day as the supreme classic of Arabic literature? Or are we referring to the moral commandments and laws with which Islam has uprooted the primitive life of the Arabs.

So, When we talk about Islam we are not talking about a single cause, indeed we are not even talking about a religion in the limited sense of the word. Islam is a way of life encompassing the spiritual, moral, economic, political and aesthetic facets. And though it retained some of the compatible pre - Islamic Arab culture patterns, since Islam was not after change for the sake of change, it has created a new culture and cilivization, a new outlook to life, to God and to the place of man in this universe. It is only this new complex superimposed way of life in Madinah which is responsible for the new outlook to alcoholic intoxication and to the success of the remarkable mass abstinence with negligible relapses.

CHAPTER 2

Alcoholism

What does Alcohol do?

Alcohol is considered by most medical authorities to be depressant of the central nervous system. But it is possible to "feel stimulated" from having had a drink. This because alcohol can dull or depress the higher brain centres before interfering with motor area functions. The drinker can be in control of his movement and speech, yet the areas that regulate thinking and reasoning and feeling are kept from functioning perfectly. Thus a person who is drinking wine may be more active because he is behaving in ways that are normally under control and not because he is actually stimulated.

When a person takes a drink of alcohol, it is not like a water going through a hose, nor is it like taking in a food product. There is a definite metabolic effect and yet there is no digestive process involved. The reason for this is that alcohol passes right through the walls of the stomach and small intestine. It is readily absorbed into the bloodstream, which carries it immediately to the brain and the central nervous system. Alcohol effects the human body much more quickly than the ordinary foods which must be broken down by enzymes and digested before they can pass in to the blood.

However, if a person has just eaten, the alcohol that goes to the stomach combines with the food and is absorbed into the blood stream more slowly. Because milk and meat consist largely of fat and protein, they are particularly effective in impeding absorption.

Wine and beer act more slowly than distilled liquor simply because of the smaller proportion of alcohol in them and because they contain other substances such as fruit, pulp and grain which help to slow absorption.

Basic material used in the preparation of wine

Wine is a famous liquid which is prepared through a process that ferments some seeds and fruits and change some sweet scenting herbs and vinegar into intoxication i,e, alcohol by means of some effective things which produce a particular substance that is very essential in the process of fermentation.

Abu Huraira (Allah be pleased with him) reported Allah's Messenger (peace and blessing of Allah be upon him) having said: *khamr* (wine) is prepared from the (fruit) of these two trees—datepalm and vine. *(Muslim)*.

Anas (Allah be pleased with him) reported: *Khamr* (wine) was prohibited when it was made unlawful, and we do not find wine of grapes but little, and the common thing of our wine was fresh and dry dates (*Bukhari*)

Nu'man bin Bashir (Allah be pleased with him) reported that the Messenger of Allah (Peace and blessing of Allah be upon him)said: Verily there is wine from maize and wine from barley, and wine from dry-dates and wine from dry grapes, and wine from honey. *(Abu Dawud)*.

It has been established now that the basic material in alcoholic fermentation is the same (i, e, glucose) whichever raw material is used. Grape juice contains ready glucose, but in the case of corn, glucose has to be produced by various treatments, before alcoholic fermentation can even start. So *Khamr* covers all alcoholic beverages, a view held by Shah Waliullah and almost all the *Imams*.

How are Alcoholic Beverages made?

Wine may be produced from the juices of vegetables, berries and fruits. The end results vary a great deal in taste and colour. However the most common substance from which wine is made is grapes. Much depends on the weather, moisture, sun, length of growing season and, of course, the kind of grapes. Juice is extracted from the fruit and with the introduction of yeast, chemical changes begin. The yeast changes the sugar in the fruit to alcohol and the process of fermentation starts.

Beer is a brew of cereals. Wheat, rye,rice or corn is boiled and yeast is added. Here, another substance called malt is needed. Malt is barley or other grain that has been steeped in water, allowed to sprout and then dried and powdered. In wheat, corn and other cereal grain, the sugar is in the form of starch. The malt is needed to change this starch to sugar. After that, the yeast which changes sugar to alcohol can perform its job, fermentation.

In making beer, the fermentation of the grain is interrupted. This causes less sugar to be changed to alcohol. As a result, beer contains less alcohol than wine. The varieties of beer and ale are the result of brewing with different amounts and kinds of cereals and water, plus differences in processing (as well as the addition of a small bitter fruit usually hops, which acts as a preservative and flavours the beer).

Distillation of alcohol results in gin, whisky, rum and brandy. For example, a fermented liquid is boiled This becomes steam or vapour. The vapour is recaptured, then flavoured by the liquid from which it has been boiled. A distilled beverage has a higher alcoholic content than the fermented brew from which it is made. Generally, these products are forty to fifty percent alcohol. Distilled beverages have different flavours and colour because of the distinctive qualities of the basic ingredients. Whisky is distilled from grain brews; brandy is made from grapes; rum is derived from sugar and molasses. Gin comes from grain alcohol and is flavoured with juniper berries.

Alcohol has no known discoverer or inventor. Records left by ancient civilization show that the substance has been with us for some time. Then as now, it offered man escape from his problems and was, therefore, associated with magic, ancestor worship, the supernatural and even religious rituals.

Distilled beverages were unknown in the Western world until the Middle Ages. By way of the Arabs, some experts say, the process was finally introduced to Europeans.

Some Important Kinds of Wine

In our age, wine is of many kinds having different names. Wine has been divided into particular categories in consideration of proportion of alcohol contained in them viz., brandy, whisky, rum, marteel etc. The proportion of alcohol in these wines range between 40 to 60 percent.

In *Gin Holandi*, and *Janifa* alcohol ranges between 33 to 40 percent, Whereas in *Boorat, Shiray* and *Madir* it ranges between 15 to 20 percent and light liquors like *Hook Shambania* and *Barjandi* contain 10 to 15 percent alcohol. Similarly light beers like *Eal, Boortar, Istoot* and *Meunich* contain 2 to 9 percent alcohol.

Some people drink light liquors because they provoke light intoxication and they are called by names other than wine and do not make a note that " the small quantity of thing, the great quantity of which creates intoxication, is also unlawful."[1]

The prevailing situation of conformity with the saying of the Holy Prophet (Peace and blessing of Allah be upon him): verily a

1. *Abu Dawud, Tirmidhi, Ibn Maja* and *Ahmad.*

section of my *ummah* will declare wine lawful under the garb of various names by which they will call it."[2] Therefore Allah's bondsmen should guard against wine. The Holy Qur'an say's:

فَلْيَحْذَرِ الَّذِيْنَ يُخَالِفُوْنَ عَنْ أَمْرِهِ أَنْ تُصِيْبَهُمْ فِتْنَةٌ أَوْ يُصِيْبَهُمْ عَذَابٌ أَلِيْمٌ○

> And let those who conspire to evade His order: beware lest grip of painful punishment befall them. "(24 :63)

We seek refuge in Allah against evil promptings, the mischiefs of our mind and evil of our works.

What part did Alcohol play in the primitive life?

Wine and beer played an important part in primitive life, particularly on the occasion of marriage, birth, death, rites of maturity, negotiations ands decisions.

During Roman and Byzantine times wine was the chief table beverage of the cities, while beer made from grain was popular in rural areas.

As monasteries were constructed and grew in size and needed a means of support, wine-making became an essential feature of their economy.

As time passed the "ritualistic" drinking of alcoholic beverages became secondary to social drinking. With this came a new problem: weighing the economic advantages of the production of distilled spirits against the social evil of excessive drinking.

This problem arose because alcoholic beverages became valuable export products for the mercantile countries of Western Europe which were anxious to export more than what they imported and thus accumulate gold and silver.

2. *Ahmad* on the authority of 'Ubada. b. Samit (ALLAH be pleased with him).

In 1689 the English Government prohibited the import of distilled liquors and encouraged domestic growth by licensing distilleries and later retail liquor stores at a very small fee. Drinking became easy and cheap; durunkenness, a national disgrace.

Excessive indulgence led to temperance movements, the most important of which was led by John Wesley, founder of the Methodist religion.

The situation was similar in America. The early colonizers brought their drinks with them. They believed that these spirits had health-giving qualities. Thus alcoholic beverages were in great demand in the earlier days of the New World, since it was felt a pint of ale could spur a man on to his tasks of felling forests and building villages. It was also believed that alcohol helped cure fevers, chills and snake bites.

Rum played an important part in the American history. The New England traders took rum to West Africa and exchanged it for slaves. The slaves were taken to the West Indies and traded for sugar and molasses. These in turn were taken back to New England to be used in making more rum. Rum was not only enjoyed by the New Englanders at that time, but it was a part of the web involving the shipping industry, slavery and the whole economy of the world.

The intoxicating liquor, which is the most vicious curse to humanity, is a "creature" of the human beings themselves. It has ruined innumerable lives, shattered multitudes of homes, and caused more misery to mankind than all other vices put together. If man-made laws of the civilized countries have any morality in them, they would have banned the brewing, purveying and consumption of intoxicants. But the traffic in alcoholic liquor brings them huge revenues which they dislike losing. There was a time when the United States of America had come to realise the curse and had imposed complete prohibition, but the "boot-leggers" and contrabands defeated the legislative ban which had to be repealed.

CHAPTER 3

Al-Khamr

Meaning of Al-Khamr

The drink prohibited in Islam is described as *Khamr*. The word *khamr* which is equivalent to the word liquor in English, is derived from the verb *khamara* which means "he covered, hid, or concealed." Since liquor shrouds the intellect of man, and renders it invalid for discriminating between right and wrong, it is, therefore, called *khamr*. *Khamr* is differently explained as meaning what intoxicates, of the expressed juice or grapes, or the juice of grapes when it was effervesced and thrown up froth, and become freed there from, and still, or it has common application to intoxicating expressed juice of anything, or any intoxicating thing that clouds or obscures the intellect. [1]

Another view is that *khamr* has been so termed due to the reason that it is put up in a place till it turns into wine. Turning of a drink into wine implies the change of odour. All these features appear in *khamr*.

Definition according to the Islamic Shari'ah

Wine under the term *Khamr* (خَمْرٌ) as defined by the Islamic Shari'ah implies all things which intoxicate. In *Bukhari* and *Muslim* it is reported on the authority of Ibn 'Umar (Allah be pleased with

1. Lane, *Lexicon*.

him) that Caliph 'Umar (Allah be pleased with him), in one of his Friday Sermons, defined *khamr* as everything that dulls the faculty of thinking.

Ibn 'Umar (Allah be pleased with him) reported that 'Umar (Allah be pleased with him) delivered Sermon upon the pulpit of the Messenger of Allah (peace and blessings of Allah be upon him) and said:

"O mankind! The prohibition of *khamr* (wine) has been revealed and that is made of five things: Grapes, dates, wheat, barley and honey: and *khamr* is what covers intellect. (*Bukhari* and *Muslim*)

Al-*Khamr*- Its Names and Attributes

The Arabs describe numerous names and attributes of *Khamr* (wine). Some important names and attributes are mentioned here as under:

(1) *Al-Khamr* (اَلْخَمْرُ) : The word used in the Holy Qur'an for wine or anything that intoxicates.

(2) *Al-Khandaris* (الخندريس) : Old wine prepared of wheat.

(3) *Al-Rahiq* (اَلرَّحِيق) : Strong and pure wine.

(4) *Al-Sukr* (اَلسُّكْر) : Intoxicating drink prepared from sweet grapes or fresh dates.

(5) *Al-Humayya* (اَلْحُمَيَّا) Wine that provokes passion.

(6) *Al-Qahwa* (اَلْقَهْوَةُ): A kind of wine.

(7) *Al-Sulafa* (اَلسُّلَافَةُ): First juice of grapes. It is a best kind of wine.

(8) *Al-Mudama* (اَلْمُدَامَةُ) A kind of wine.

(9) *Al-Rahu* (اَلرَّاحُ) : Wine that causes gladness and cheerfulness.

(10) *Al-Sahba'u* (اَلصَّهْبَاءُ) The red liquor.

(11) *Al-Nabidhu* (اَلنَّبِيْذُ): A kind of wine made from dates and grapes.

(12) *Al-Bit'* (اَلْبِتْعُ) : Strong wine made of honey and dates.

(13) *Al-Kumait* (اَلْكُمَيْتُ) Ruddy wine.

(14) *Al-Sakurka* (اَلسَّكُرْكَةُ) A kind of wine.

(15) *Al-Fadikh* (اَلْفَضِيْخُ) A wine made of the juice of grapes; date - wine.

(16) *Al-'Uqar* (اَلْعُقَارُ) : Wine that stupefies.

(17) *Al-Qarqaf* (اَلْقَرْقَفُ) Wine, cold drink.

(18) *Al-Zalla* (اَلطَّلَاءُ) : A kind of wine.

(19) *Al-Isfant* (الاسفنط) : An aromatic wine.

(20) *Al-Muzaffat* (اَلْمُزَفَّتُ) A kind of wine.

(21) *Al-Safaqa* (اَلصَّفْقَةُ): A kind of wine.

(22) *Al-Atiq'* (اَلْعَاتِقُ) : Old wine having bitter taste and strong intoxication.

(23) *Al-Badhiq* (اَلْبَاذِقُ) : A drink made from juice of grapes slightly boiled.

(24) *Al-Tila'* (الطّلَاءُ) : Wine prepared from teckened juice of grapes.

(25) *Al-Musha'sha'a* (اَلْمُشَعْشَعَةُ): A kind of wine.

(26) *Al- Muqdiyya* (اَلْمُقْدِيَّةُ) : A delicious and fragrant drink.

(27) *Al-Shamul* (اَلشَّمُوْلُ) : A fresh wine.

(28) *Al-Mizr* (اَلْمِزْرُ) : Abyssinian beer: beverage made of millet, barley or grain.

(29) *Al-Mustar* (اَلْمُصْطَارُ) A kind of wine.

(30) *Al-Mara'* (اَلْمَرَاءُ) : A kind of wine.

(31) *Al-Qummahan* (اَلْقُمَّهَانُ) : literally : Scum over the surface of old wine

(32) *Al-Khurtum* (اَلْخُرْطُومُ) A kind of wine.

(33) *Al-Qindid* (اَلْقِنْدِيْدُ) A kind of wine perfumed with musk.

(34) *Al-Ja'atu* (اَلْجُعَّةُ) : Beer.

(35) *Al-Ithmu* (اَلاِثْمُ) : A kind of wine.

The Holy Qur'an has made a mention of some of these kinds of wine:

1. *Al-Khamr* : It is the most famous and common name of wine because drinking *khamr* brings about a number of harms and troubles.

2. *Al-Sukr* : Wine has been termed as *sukr* because it has the effect of intoxication.

3. *Al-Rahiq* : It is a wine, clear, pure and old,. This word has been used as a characteristic of the wine of Paradise in the following Qur'anic verse:

يُسْقَوْنَ مِنْ رَّحِيقٍ مَّخْتُومٍ.

"They are given therein (Paradise) to drink of a pure wine, sealed."

(83 : 25)

The word *Khamr* has appeared six times in the Holy Qur'an : Once in subjective case in verse 5 : 90, twice in objective case in verses 12 : 36, 41 and thrice in genetive case in verses 2 : 219, 5 : 91 and 47 : 15. The Holy Prophet (peace and blessing of Allah be upon him) has named wine as :

Ummul Khaba'ith (اُمُّ الْخَبَائِثْ) The fountainhead of evils.

Ummul fawahish (أُمُّ الْفَوَاحِشِ) : The origin of all sorts of atrocities.

Akbarul Kaba'ir (اَكْبَرُ الْكَبَائِرِ) : The most heinous of major sins.

Ra'su kulli khatia (رَأْسُ كُلِّ خَطِيْئَةٍ) The head of all errors and lapses.

Miftahu kulli sharr (مِفْتَاحُ كُلِّ شَرٍّ) The key to all evils and mischiefs.

The Holy Prophet (peace and blessing of Allah be upon him) has attributed these names to *Khamr* (wine) because it embodies all the above characteristics.

Abstinents in the Pre-Islamic Arabia

According to the History of Arabia, the first man who abandoned wine in the pre-Islamic period was Walid b. Mughira who visualised its harms. Another report mentions the name of Qais b. 'Asim. Some other persons who avoided drinking wine before the advent of Islam were:

Muqis b. Sababa, 'Abdul Muttalib — the grandfather of our Holy Prophet (peace and blessings of Allah be upon him) Abu Talib— father of Hadrat 'Ali (Allah be pleased with him), Qusayy b. Kilab, Warqa b. Naufal— the uncle of Hadrat Khadija (Allah be pleased with her) -Shaiba b. Rabi'a and 'Abbas b. Maradas.

It is reported that people said to 'Abbas b. Maradas, "Why don't you drink wine while it increases warmth?" He replied, " I am not going to hold my ignorance in my hand and put it into my stomach, nor do I like to be the leader of a people in the morning and turn to be a foolish one in the evening." These words are of a man who lived in the age of ignorance and had great regard for reason and nobility. He did not like lowliness and insanity. What a wisdom which these words impart ! Is there any soul to receive exhortation?

In the similar way, the prominent Companions of the Holy Prophet (peace and blessing of Allah be upon him), like Hadrat Abu Bakr, Hadrat 'Uthman and Hadrat 'Ali (Allah be pleased with them) abstained from drinking wine during the pre-Islamic period. Hadrat 'Uthman (Allah be pleased with him) was asked why he had not touched alcohol even during his pre-Islamic life. His answer was "*al khamr* robs the mind totally ; and I have not yet seen anything which when entirely 'robbed or curtailed will come back in its original intact form."[2] Another contemporary of Hadrat 'Uthman (Allah be pleased with him) refused to drink wine. He said," I refuse to consume that which consumes my mind." [3]

The Holy Qur'an on the prohibition of Al-Khamr

The verses of the Holy Qur'an which touched the problem are:

يَسْئَلُونَكَ عَنِ الْخَمْرِ وَالْمَيْسِرِ ط قُلْ فِيْهِمَا إِثْمٌ كَبِيْرٌ وَّ مَنَافِعُ
لِلنَّاسِ وَ اِثْمُهُمَا اَكْبَرُ مِنْ نَّفْعِهِمَا ط

"They ask thee (O Prophet) about *Khamr* (intoxicants) and games of chance (gambling). Say:In both of them there is great harm althought there are some advantages as well in them for men, but their harm is much greater than their advantages." (2:219)

يَا اَيُّهَا الَّذِيْنَ أٰمَنُوْا لاَ تَقْرَبُوْا الصَّلٰوةَ وَأَنْتُمْ سُكَارٰى حَتّٰى تَعْلَمُوْا
مَاتَقُوْلُوْنَ

"O ye who believe ! Draw not near unto Prayer when you are in a state of intoxication until you know what you utter." (4:43)

يَااَيُّهَا الَّذِيْنَ اٰمَنُوْا اِنَّمَا الْخَمْرُ وَالْمَيْسِرُ وَ الْاَ نْصَابُ وَالْاَزْلاَمُ
رِجْسٌ مِّنْ عَمَلِ الشَّيْطَانِ فَاجْتَنِبُوْهُ لَعَلَّكُمْ تُفْلِحُوْنَ. اِنَّمَا يُرِيْدُ
الشَّيْطَانُ أَنْ يُّوْقِعَ بَيْنَكُمُ الْعَدَاوَةَ وَالْبَغْضَاءَ فِيْ الْخَمْرِ وَالْمَيْسِرِ
وَيَصُدَّكُمْ عَنْ ذِكْرِاللّٰهِ وَعَنِ الصَّلٰوةِ فَهَلْ أَنْتُمْ مُّنْتَهُوْنَ.

2. Al-Nuwairi, op. cit., Vol. p. 84 3. Ibid.

"O believers! Surely wine and games of chance, (ungodly) shrines, and divining devices are abomination of Satan's work. Avoid them, that ye may prosper. Only would Satan sow hatred and strife among you, by wine, and games of chance, and turn to aside from the remembrance of Allah, and from Prayer: Will you not therefore, abstain from them? (5:90, 91).

From the foregoing Qur'anic verses we can deduce that all intoxicants resulting into loss of wit, wastage of wealth and ruin of health, debauching status and nobility and marring personality, are unlawful like wine, opium, hemp etc. All these substances are unlawful in *Shari'ah*, whether they are smelt, snuffed or drunk.

Traditions on Prohibition of Al-Khamr

Though originally the Arabic word "*Khamr*" meant only wine, it is also applied to all the liquors brewed from wheat, barley, dried grapes, dates and honey. Whatever is the material from which liquor is prepared and whatever is the process of preparation, every intoxicant is forbidden. The Holy Prophet (Peace and blessing of Allah be upon him) prohibited all sorts of intoxicants and there are Traditions that clearly testify this: "Every intoxicant is wine and is unlawful. "Every drink that intoxicates is unlawful . "I prohibit every intoxicant."

Every Intoxicant is Unlawful

'Abdullah bin 'Amr (Allah be pleased with him) reported that the Holy Prophet (Peace and blessings of Allah be upon him) prohibited intoxicants, games of chance, card playing and *Gobairah*[4] and he said: Every intoxicant is unlawful. *(Abu Dawud)*

Ibn 'Umar (Allah be pleased with him) reported that the Messenger of Allah (peace and blessing of Allah be upon him) said: Every intoxicant is *Khamr* and every intoxicant is forbidden. He who

4. *Gobairah* is a kind of wine.

drinks wine in this world and dies while he is addicted to it not having repented, will not be given a drink in the Hereafter. *(Muslim)*

'A'isha (Allah be pleased with her) reported that the Prophet of Allah (peace and blessings of Allah be upon him) was asked about *Bit'*[5], whereupon he said: Every drink that causes intoxication is forbidden. (*Agreed upon*)

Umm Salama (Allah be pleased with her) reported that the Prophet of Allah (peace and blessings of Allah be upon him) prohibited every intoxicant and exciting food. *(Abu Dawud)*

Abu Musa (Allah be pleased with him) reported Allah's Apostle (peace and blessings of Allah be upon him) sent me and Mu'adh bin Jabal (Allah be pleased with him) to Yaman. I said: Allah's Apostle in our land wine is prepared out of barley which is known as *Mizr* (beer of our times) and also from honey which is known as *Bit'*(are these also forbidden?), whereupon he said: Every intoxicant is forbidden. *(Muslim)*

Abu Burda (Allah be pleased with him) reported on the authority of his grand father that Allah's Apostle (peace and blessing of Allah be upon him) sent him and Mu'adh bin Jabal to Yaman and said to them: Give glad tidings to the (people) and make things easy (for them) teach (them), and do not repel (them);and I think he also said: co-operate cheerfully with each other. When he (the Holy Prophet) turned his back Abu Musa (Allah be pleased with him) turning towards him, said: Allah's Apostle, they (the people of Yaman) have a drink which is made from honey and that is prepared by cooking it until it coagulates, and *Mizr* is prepared from barley, whereupon Allah's Messenger (peace and blessings of Allah be upon him) said; Every *Askara* (intoxicant) that detains you from Prayer is forbidden. *(Muslim)*

---

5. Bit' is an intoxicating drink made of honey.

Here the word "*Askara*" (intoxicant) has very comprehensive and meaningfull expression that covers so many shades of meanings connected with the use of wine. It may mean the intoxicant which keeps us away from Prayer as we read in the Qur'an:[6]

لَاتَقْرَبُوْا الصَّلٰوةَ وَأَنْتُمْ سُكَارَى ،

"Draw not near unto prayer when you are in a state of intoxication." (4 : 43)

The state of intoxication is thus described as an obstacle in the way of Prayer.

This expression may also mean that intoxicants make one unmindful of Prayer as we find in the Qur'an.

إِنَّمَا يُرِيْدُ الشَّيْطَانُ أَن يُوْقِعَ بَيْنَكُمُ الْعَدَاوَةَ وَالْبَغْضَاءَ فِي الْخَمْرِ وَالْمَيْسِرِ وَيَصُدَّكُمْ عَنْ ذِكْرِاللهِ وَعَنِ الصَّلٰوةِ

"By means of intoxicants and games of chance, Satan seeks only to sow enmity and hatred amongst you, and to turn you away from the remembrance of Allah and from Prayer." (5:91)

This expression may also imply the drink that clouds the intellect and consciousness of a person so that he fails to keep himself devoted in Prayer. In prayer man faces Allah spiritually during his earthly life; he is, therefore, required to have full consciousness of his own self, of the act of devotion in which he is engaged and of the Great Lord with Whom he is in spiritual communion at that time. Consciousness is indispensable in every act of worship which is destroyed under the influence of an intoxicant should be in his senses to be aware of what he rehearses.

---

6. The word *sukr* سُکر (state of intoxication) used in the Arabic text implies that this Commandment prohibits not only drinking but every kind of intoxicant. Moreover, though every intoxicating thing is unlawful, the offence of intoxication is doubled and becomes much more heinous, when Prayer is offered in such a state.

(S. Abul A'la Maududi, *The Meaning of the Qur'an*, Vol. II, pp. 125, 126).

Jabir (Allah be pleased with him) reported that a person came from Jaishan, a town of Yaman, and he asked Allah's Apostle (peace and blessings of Allah be upon him) about the wine which was drunk in his country and which was prepared from millet and was called *Mizr*. Allah's Apostle (peace and blessings of Allah be upon him) asked him whether that was intoxicating. He replied in affirmative. Thereupon Allah's Apostle (peace and blessings of Allah be upon him) said: Every intoxicant is forbidden. Verily Allah, the Exalted and Majestic, made a convenant to those who drank intoxicants to make them drink *Tinat al-Khabal*. They said: O' Allah's Prophet what is *Tinat al-Khabal*? He (the Holy Prophet) replied:It is the sweat of the denizens of Hell the discharge of the denizens of Hell. *(Muslim)*

Nafi' reported Ibn 'Umar as saying: Allah's Apostle (peace and blessings of Allah be upon him) has said: Every intoxicant is *khamr* and every *khamr* is forbidden. *(Muslim)*

This hadith clearly shows that all kinds of intoxicants, e.g., opium, hemp and cocaine are forbidden. Imam Ibn Taimiyya has stated:

> "Hemp is forbidden whether it clouds intellect or not. Immoral persons are used to it...So whoso use hemp are like those who drink wine as its effects are nearly the same." [7]

Intoxicant even in Smallest Quantity is Unlawful

Some people think that a small quantity of alcohol can do no harm. But it is one of the myths which the scientific analysis has already exploded. Even such a tiny concentration of alcohol in blood as 0.15% (*i.e.*, one-seventh of one per cent) impairs the faculties so much that driving becomes extremely dangerous. Also, it requires a strong will power to restrict a drunkard's intake of alcohol. As the alcohol destroys the power of judgment, as it frees man from every

7. Ibn Taimiyya, *Fatawa*, Vol. IV, p. 262.

inhibition, it is foolish to believe that once started a man can control his drinking habits. When the will power is weakened by the effect of alcohol, drinking leads to drunkenness and finally to alcoholism. Islam does not tend a man into this trap. It was for this reason that the Holy Prophet(peace and blessings of Allah be upon him laid down the principle: If a large quantity of something is intoxicant, then even its smallest portion is also unlawful, and if a cup of anything is intoxicant, them even a drop of it is also unlawful.

Jabir (Allah be pleased with him) reported that the Apostle of Allah (peace and blessings of Allah be upon him) said: What intoxicates in greater quantity is unlawful also in small quantity.

(Tirmidhi, Abu Dawud, Ibn Maja)

'A'isha (Allah be pleased with her) reported from the Messenger of Allah (peace and blessings of Allah be upon him) who said: What is intoxicating upto *Farq*[8] is unlawful even in its handful.

(Tirmidhi, Dawud, Ahmad)

Two points should be clearly borne in mind in this connection:

(a) Anything that causes intoxication is forbidden in Islam, whether its quantity is large or small. No person can argue that since the small quantity of any intoxicant does not affect the mind adversely, it may not be treated as unlawful. This is a fallacious reasoning. It is the intoxicant which is unlawful, no matter whatever be its quantity. The *haram* is *haram* and a Muslim should be scrupulous enough to abstain from it, whether its quantity is large or small.

(b) Secondly, no person can say that since the use of liquor does not intoxicate him, he is justified in using that. If a habitual drunkard does not lose control over himself altogether, it does not mean that the liquor ceases to be forbidden. Islam has made

8. '*Farq*' means eight seers.

certain foods and drinks unlawful primarily on the basis of the pernicious effects that these create on the spiritual and moral health of human beings. Drinking is an evil through and through — the undesirable fact which is recognised by all right-thinking people whether they belong to our age or to the old age. It saps the very root of morality, self-control and God-consciousness, making man an easy prey to evil.

A Drunkard is not a Believer

Abu Huraira (Allah be pleased with him) reported that the Apostle of Allah (peace and blessings of Allah be upon him) said: "An adulterer, at the time he is committing illegal sexual intercourse is not a believer; and a person, at the time of drinking wine is not a believer, and a theif, at time of stealing, is not a believer. *(Bukhari)*

A Habitual Drunkard will not Enter Paradise

Ibn 'umar (Allah be pleased with him) reported that the Apostle of Allah (peace and blessings of Allah be upon him) said: There are three for whom paradise has been prohibited — a habitual drunkard, one disobedient to parents, and a careless husband and who establishes impurity in his family. *(Ahmad, Nisa'i)*

Abu Musa al-Ash'ari (Allah be pleased with him) reported that the Apostle of Allah (peace and blessings of Allah be upon him) said: there are three (categories of persons) who will not enter Paradise-a habitual drunkard, one who cuts off blood-ties and one who believes in sorcery. *(Ahmad)*

Abu Umama (Allah be pleased with him) reported that the Apostle of Allah (peace and blessings of Allah be upon him) said: Verily, the Almighty Allah sent me as a mercy for all the worlds; and my Almighty, the Glorious Lord, ordered me to abolish drums, musical instruments, idols, cross and the affairs of the Days of Ignorance. My Allah Almighty, the Glorious, has promised : By My honour, out of My servants who drinks a cup of wine but I will give him drink like it from hot water (of Hell); and one who gives it up out of My fear but I will give him drink from the Holy Fountain. *(Ahmad)*

The Cursed Ten Persons

Anas (Allah be pleased with him) reported that the Holy Prophet (peace and blessings of Allah be upon him) said: Verily Allah has cursed ten persons — one who squeezes it; one who is engaged for squeezing it; one who drinks it; one who carries it; one to whom it is carried; one who serves drink; one who sells it; one who devours its price; one who purchases it and one for whom it is purchased.

(Tirmidhi, Abu Dawud, Ibn Maja)

Wine is a Disease

In medicines, wine should be avoided because wine itself is a disease:

Wa'il al-Hadrami (Allah be pleased with him) reported that Tariq ibn Suwaid al-ju'fi asked the Holy Prophet (peace and blessings of Allah be upon him), about liquor. He forbade (its use) and he expressed hatred that it should be prepared. He (Tariq) said: I prepare it as a medicine, whereupon he (the Holy Prophet) said: It is no medicine, but an ailment. *(Muslim)*

Wine Should Not be Offered as a Gift

The Holy Prophet (peace and blessings of Allah be upon him) did not permit wine to be offered to non-Muslims as a gift. It was declared forbidden.

Some of the Muslims said: Why spill it, why not give it to the Jews? Thereupon the Holy Prophet (peace and blessings of Allah be upon him) said: He who made it unlawful has also forbidden it to be offered as a gift to other people.

No Excuse for Wine-drinking

Cold climate is no excuse for wine-drinking:

Dailamah al-Humairi (Allah be pleased with him) reported : I asked: O' Messenger of Allah, verily we are in a cold land, and we have to do hard labour therein, and we prepare wine from this wheat which gives us strength in our works and in the chill of our cities. He sad: Does it intoxicate? 'Yes,said I. He said : Give it up. I said: Verily the people can not give it up. He said: If they do not give it up, fight with them. *(Abu Dawud)*

A Drunkard is a Worshipper of Idol

Abu Huraira (Allah be pleased with him) reported that the Holy Prophet (peace and blessings of Allah be upon him), said:One who is addicted to wine is like one who worships idols. *(Ahmad & Nisai)*

Ibn'Abbas (Allah be pleased with him) reported that the Messenger of Allah (peace and blessings of Allah be upon him), said: If the habitual drunkard dies, he meets Allah like one who worships idols. *(Ahmad, Ibn Maja)*

The Traditions mentioned above are enough testimony to prove that every intoxicant is *khamr* and every *khamr* is a *haram* (unlawful). If the large quantity of a thing causes intoxication, its small quantity even if it does not provoke intoxication, is also *haram* (unlawful). Thus everything which causes intoxication is unlawful.

Khamr is a key to all evils and a mainspring of all atrocities.

May Allah safeguard us against the blind pursuit of evil promptings and against the obeisance of Satan.

Prohibition of Wine in Islam — Brief History

Historians differ about the period during which wine was declared unlawful. Some hold that it was declared unlawful in the month of Rabi'ul Awwal, 4 A. H. (August, 625 A. D.) after the battle of Banu Nadir while the other contend that wine was declared unlawful after the battle of Ahzab (Tribes) which was fought in the month of Shawwal, 4 A.H. (March, 625 A.D.) It is also said that battle of Ahzab was fought in the month of Shawwal, 5 A.H. (February, 626 A.D.)

The first view is more authentic due to the narration of Hadrat 'Abdullah b. 'Umar (Allah be pleased with him) wherein he reported: "I volunteered myself to the Holy Prophet (peace and blessings of Allah be upon him) on the day of battle of Uhud while I was still a lad of 14 years and he rejected me; and I (again) offered myself to him on the day of battle of *Khandaq* (Trench) while I was a lad of 15 years and he allowed me to participate in the battle of Trench. This tradition has been transmitted by *Bukhari* and *Muslim* and we come to learn that there was only a gap of one year between the battle of Uhud and the battle of Trench and the battle of Uhud according to the consensus of opinion of the historians, took place in the month of Shawwal 3 A. H.

There are still some other historians who hold the view that wine was declared unlawful in the year of Treaty of Hudaibiya. THis event occured in the month of Dhi Qa'da, 6 A. H. (March 627 A. D.) It is not possible to reconcile these three historic reports. It is said that wine was declared unlawful gradually, as everyone is aware, in three different stages. Most probably, the first report deals with the period of revelation of the Qur'anic Verse: "They ask thee (O' Prophet) about *khamr* (intoxicants) and games of change (gambling). Say : In both of them there is great harm........" (2: 219), whereas the second report of history indicates the period of revelation of the Verse: "O' ye who believe! Draw not near unto Prayer when you are in a state of intoxication until you know what you utter". (4: 43) The third report perhaps pertains to the revelation of the Verse: "O' ye who believe! Surely wine and games of chance, (ungodly) shrines, and

divining devices, are abomination of Satan's work. Avoi
ye may prosper." (5: 90: 91). With the revelation of these tv
drinking wine was completely banned. To sum up, wine v
declared as unlawful in the month of Rabi'ul Awwal, 4 A. H. (August 625 A.D.) For the second time it was declared unlawful in the month of Shawwal, 4 A. H. (March, 626 A.D.) It was declared unlawful on the third occasion in the month of Dhi-Qa'da (March 627 A.D.)

The Background to Revelation of Verses on the Unlawfulness of Wine

Ibn Mardawiya reported that Hadrat Sa'd b. Abi Waqqas (Allah be pleased with him) said: (The Verse concerning) unlawfulness of wine was revealed in my favour. A person from amongst the *Ansar* (Helpers) prepared a meal and invited us to it. People attended the function and drank till they were intoxicated by the consumption of wine— this incident occured before the unlawfulness of wine was revealed. They vied in boasting, with one another. The *Ansar* (Helpers) said: "*Ansar* are best." The Quraishites said, "The Quraishites are excellent." Thereupon, a man stretched his hand towards the bit of a camel and struck at its nose and cut it. I came to the Holy Prophet (peace and blessings of Allah be upon him) and mentioned it to him. Upon this the Verse of *Sura Ma'ida* concerning the prohibition of wine was revealed.

'Abdullah b. Husnaid, Ibn Jarir, Ibn Mundhir, Baihaqi and Ibn Mardawiya have reported Ibn 'Abbas (Allah be pleased with him) as saying: Verily, the (Verse concerning) unalwfulness of wine was revealed in favour of two tribes of *Ansar* who had drunk wine. As they were intoxicated they scoffed at one another. On regaining their senses, one of them began to realise the sign (of nonsense) on his face, head and beard. He said: "That person has done this nonsense with me. By Allah, had he been kind and mericful he would not have done this with me", till rancour against one another took root in their hearts. On this Allah revealed this Verse of *Sura al-Ma'ida.* *(5: 90, 91)*

It is also reported that Hadrat 'Abdur Rahman b. Auf (Allah be pleased with him) arranged meal and wine and invited some Companions of the Holy Prophet (peace and blessings of Allah be upon him), when wine was not yet prohibited. They ate and drank. When they were intoxicated and the time of sunset Prayer approached, one of them left for Prayer and recited *Sura al-Kafirun* (Disbelievers) wrongly thus: "say: 'O disbelievers, I worship not that which you worship and we worship that which you worship.' Upon this the Verse was revealed and drinking wine at the time of Prayer was prohibited. They took wine at night till the main Verse of *Sura al-Ma'ida* pertaining to unlawfulness of wine was revealed.

It should be borne in mind that in the first Tradition, it was Hadrat Sa'd b. Abi Waqqas (Allah be pleased with him) who had reported the trouble that had occured to him. The second Tradition, however, furnished a report of an incident that instead of Sa'd b. Abi Waqqas, occured between the people of two tribes of *Ansar*. In both the Traditions one and the same incident has been reported. This discussion resolves the inconsistency between the two Traditions. As far the last Tradition, it reports an event that was common amongst the people which attributed to the revelation of the Verse containing the Divine Command about the unlawfulness of wine.

Among all these factors leading to the prohibition of wine was the prayer of Hadrat 'Umar (Allah be pleased with him) : "Our Allah, furnish unto us a manifest verdict about the (legal status of wine)."

Gradual Prohibition of Khamr in Islam

It was very difficult for the Arabs to give up drinking wine. Therefore, the Islamic *Shari'ah* adopted a gradual course in declaring wine as unlawful. The prohibition of *Khamr* came in several stages.

The first Qur'anic Verse in which there was a mention of alcoholic intoxicants was revealed late in Makkah, before, the Holy Prophet (peace and blessings of Allah be upon him) emigrated to Madinah. It only touched the problem lightly. The Holy Qur'an says:

وَمِنْ ثَمَرَاتِ النَّخِيْلِ وَالأَعْنَابِ تَتَّخِذُوْنَ مِنْهُ سَكَرًا وَّ رِزْقًا حَسَنًا

> "And of the fruits of the date-palms and grapes, —ye obtain from them intoxicants and goodly provision." *(16: 67)*

Many interpretations of this Verse have been offered. According to one of the various commentaries the word *Sukr* (state of intoxicants) implies *Khamr* (all kinds of intoxicants). This Verse was revealed before wine was declared unlawful. later on this Verse was superseded by the Verse of *Sura al-Ma'ida*. *(5:90,91)*

There is another interpretation of this Verse according to which *Sukr* implies *nabith* which is not considered wine according to the opinion of some of the Hanafite scholars and that is prepared by cooking the juice of dates and grapes till one-third of the ingeredients is left. For this reason, the said Verse of *Sura al-Nahl* has not been abrogated.

According to still another interpretation Sukr means wine but the word *Sukr* is used *vis-a-vis* "excellent providence" (*al rizq-ul-hasan*). Moreever providence has been characterised as excellent in the Verse but *Sukr* has been left un-defined. This furnishes a formidable argument to those who believe in the abrogation of the Verse and hold *Sukr* unlawful because *Sukr* contain no excellence and is devoid of good and every thing of this nature is abominable.

This Verse implies that the juice of the fruits of date-palms and vines contains two things. One is that which is pure and wholesome food for man and the other is that which turns into alcohol after it becomes rotten. But it has been left to the choice of man to obtain pure, healthy food from this providence or to drink it as intoxicant wine to excite him and make him lose his self-control. This also contains a hint as to the prohibition of wine. [9]

Intoxicants are spoken of here in contrast with goodly provision in the early revelations. The verse speaks of strong drink as something different from good nourishment. For some sensitive Muslims like'Umar ibn al-Khattab (Allah be pleased with him), this Verse was enough to raise suspicion about the wisdom and purity of intake of *Khamr*. 'Umar (Allah be pleased with him) himself had been well known for his heavy drinking and his drunken aggressive episodes during his pre-Islamic life and as such he was probably very sensitive to its evils.[10]

Some of these perceptive Muslims went out of their way to ask the Holy Prophet(peace and blessings of Allah be upon him) about the righteousness of continuing to take *khamr*. A few of them must have started to reduce their rate of drinking or even to begin their abstinence efforts in spite of the fact of that drinking was still not forbidden religiously.

In the second stage the issue was treated in a more direct yet cautious manner. The Qur'anic Verse was revealed in *Madinah* and it came as an answer to the questions which these Muslims had raised about *khamr* and games of chance. The Holy Qur'an says:

يَسْئَلُوْنَكَ عَنِ الْخَمْرِ وَالْمَيْسِرِ ط قُلْ فِيْهِمَا اِثْمٌ كَبِيْرٌ وَّ مَنَا فِعُ
لِلنَّاسِ وَاِثْمُهُمَا اَكْبَرُ مِنْ نَّفْعِهِمَا ط

"They ask thee (O Prophet) about *khamr* (intoxicants) and game of chance (gambling) Say: In both of them there is great harm although there is some advantage as well in them for men, but their harm is much greater than their advantages. *(2: 219)*

9. S. Abul A'la Maududi, *The Meaning of the Qur'an*, Vol. VI, p. 79.

10. Sayyid Qutb, *Fi Zilal Al-Qur'an*, Vol. III, p. 33.

At this stage, people continued to drink wine for its petty benefits while a majority of the people abandoned it for its being a great sin. Undoubtedly everything that entails a great sin and promise little benefit, is harmful and hence unlawful. In this Verse a mere disapproval of alcoholic and intoxicating drinks was pronounced to serve as preliminary to their final prohibition. It clearly gives support to the people whose acquired refined piousness had made them perceive a great sin in *Khamr* even before they were told about it. However, because this verse had not prohibited the intake, of *Khamr*, the majority of Muslims continued to drink, particularly in the morning and late afternoon or evening as the custom dictated. But, as one would expect many more people would have started to reduce their daily consumption and many more would have developed some guilt feeling towards drinking something which had sin.

Allah, the Exalted, has declared murder, concealing evidence and slander as sin but none of these sins has been treated as a great sin except the sin of drinking and polythesism because polytheism has been defined as a great sin:

وَمَنْ يُّشْرِكْ بِاللّٰهِ فَقَدِ افْتَرَىٰ إِثْمًا عَظِيْمًا

"Whosoever ascribes partners to Allah hath indeed forged a tremendous sin." *(4:48)*

There is no room for any doubt that this Verse is an authority on the unlawfulness of drinking wine in the sight of wise and prudent persons.

When the Muslim society was ready for the next morsel, the third step came with still greater restrictions. At this stage Muslims were prohibited from coming to Mosque while drunk. The Holy Qur'an says:

يَا أَيُّهَا الَّذِيْنَ اٰمَنُوْا لَا تَقْرَبُوا الصَّلٰوةَ وَأَنْتُمْ سُكَارٰى حَتّٰى تَعْلَمُوْا مَاتَقُوْلُوْنَ

"O ye who believe! draw not near unto prayer when you are in a state of intoxication until you know that you utter." *(4:43)*

The earlier Commandment (2:219) was that drinking is an evil thing and Allah does not approve of it. Accordingly some of the Muslims began to refrain from it since that time. The majority of them, however, did not give it up and often offered prayer in a state of intoxication and they muddled and faltered in their recitation. probably this Commandment came in the beginning of 4 A.H. and prohibited the offering of prayer while one was drunk. As a result of this, the Companions changed the timings of their drinking to avoid clash with the timings of prayers.[11]

The Verse was revealed after one of the Muslim emigrants (from Makkah), who had been leading the evening prayer as an Imam, had been unable to recite correctly the Qur'anic Verses he had read aloud in prayer.[12] He had been too drunk to recite correctly.

Drunkenness was now placed face to face in a direct encounter with prayer, Islam's most important act of worship. The Holy Prophet (peace and blessings of Allah be upon him) says: "prayer is the pillar of religion. The one who performs it has established his religion and the one who abandoned it has ruined (his) religion." That is why some Muslim theologians consider a person who discontinues saying his prayers as a renegade (*Murtad*).

On the revelation of this Divine injunction, the Muslims abandoned drinking at the time of prayer. The hours of daily five prayers mostly fall in day time and partly at night. Therefore, whosoever holds back his hands from drinking near prayer hours, will definitely avoid intoxicants during the whole time lest the prayer hours should arrive while he is in a state of intoxication.

Now the pioneer Muslim city state was ready for the final step in hierarchy of collective abstinence.

---

11. S. Abul A'la Maududi, *The Meaning of Qur'an*, Vol. II, p. 125.
12. Al-Imam Ahmad Ibn Hanbal as quoted by Ibn Kathir.

Most of its addicts and heavy drinkers had overcome their withdrawal symptoms and had developed the more sober habit of social drinking. Many became abstinent. The few who continued to have sporadic bouts of heavy drinking were now a tiny minority which harboured the shame and guilt of missing prayers in the Mosque whenever they were drunk. Such a minority was however psychologically ready to comply with a Commandment which completely banned *Khamr*. This would terminate the conflict and vacillation in which they lived and end their guilt. And so came the final Commandment about total prohibition of *al-Kharm:*

يَا اَيُّهَا الَّذِيْنَ اٰمَنُوْا اِنَّمَا الْخَمْرُ وَالْمَيْسِرُ وَالْاَنْصَابُ وَالْاَزْلَامُ
رِجْسٌ مِّنْ عَمَلِ الشَّيْطَانِ فَاجْتَنِبُوْهُ لَعَلَّكُمْ تُفْلِحُوْنَ. اِنَّمَا يُرِيْدُ
الشَّيْطَانُ اَنْ يُّوْقِعَ بَيْنَكُمُ الْعَدَاوَةَ وَالْبَغْضَاءَ فِى الْخَمْرِ وَالْمَيْسِرِ
وَيَصُدَّكُمْ عَنْ ذِكْرِ اللّٰهِ وَعَنِ الصَّلٰوةِ فَهَلْ اَنْتُمْ مُّنْتَهُوْنَ.

> "O' believers! surely wine and games of chance, (ungodly) shrines, and divining devices, are an abomination of Satan's work. Aviod them, that ye may prosper. only would Satan sow hatred and strife among you, by wine, and games of chance, and trun you aside from the remembrance of Allah, and from prayer: Will you not, therefore, abstain from them?" (5:90,91)

Thus the remarkable quick response of "We have desisted O' Allah," came after three years of gradual social and ethical control of collective moral and spiritual "reciprocal inhibition" of drunkenness. Whenever the spiritual and moral influence of one step reached its climax, the Muslims were moved to the next step until the miracle of collective abstinence became a reality. So each stage in the collective hierarchy revealed to the whole nation was like a set of many graded steps to the individual.

Individual difference among Muslims caused some of them to plunge into immediate abstinence from the very first step and others to postpone it till the last prohibition, but they were all ready to accept whole-heartedly the final Commandment of prohibition.

The final Commandment with respect to the prohibition of wine spread fast from house to house and as the Call, "Surely Al-*Khamr* has been forbidden" echoed through the corners of *Madinah*, pots, jars and leather skins full of liquor were broken or emptied in every house till liquor flowed in the lanes of *Madinah*.

In the Mosque of *Madinah*, the Prophet (peace and blessings of Allah be upon him was reciting the verses of the Holy Qur'an proclaiming to humanity the banning of all types of *Khamr*. A large group of the faithfuls listened attentively in transcendental silence. When the Holy Prophet (peace and blessings of Allah be upon him) finished his recitation the group of faithful listeners replied to the Qur'anic revelation with one determined voice, "We have desisted, O' Allah,""We have desisted, O' our God." [13]

The Prophet (peace and blessings of Allah be upon him then walked with his beloved Companions Abu Bakr and 'Umar (Allah be pleased with them) to a pre-designated part of the city where other groups of people were told to drink their store of *Khamr*. "Do you know what this is? " The Prophet Muhammad (peace and blessings of Allah be upon him) asked the crowd, pointing to the skins and large leather post full of alcoholic drink. "Yes, O' Messenger of Allah," the crowd chorused, "this is *Khamr*" "You said the truth," the Prophet (peace and blessings of Allah be upon him) proclaimed (his famous Hadith), "Surely Allah has cursed al-*Khamr* and cursed the one who brews it and the one for whom it is brewed, the one who drinks it and the one who serves it, the one who buys and the one who consumes (profits from) its price."[14]

The Holy Prophet (peace and blessings of Allah be upon him

13. Quoted by Imam Ahmad Ibn Hanbal, Ibn Kathir, op. cit., Vol. II, p. 636.

14. Quoted by 'Abdullah Ibn 'Umar, Ibn Kathir, ibid., pp. 640, 641.

then ordered for a sharp knife with which he cut open the cool glutted skins and leather containers so that the liquid burst out and flooded the soil. He refused to accept the assistance offered by 'Umar (Allah be pleased with him) in piercing the leather skins and insisted on doing the whole job with his blessed hands.

One of his Companions said that those leather skins and containers might be of use in keeping liquids other than *Khamr* and urged against their destruction. The Prophet (peace and blessings of Allah be upon him) however, continued cutting open the skins and replied with a tinge of emotion in his gentle rather husky voice, "Yes, they may be of some use but I surely do this to express my abhorrence against something that Allah has cursed."[15]

Wine merchants who brought their commodity to Madinah from places as far away as Syria, submitted to the new Commandment. They condemmed their precious drink. They could neither sell it, nor drink it, nor even give it away. It had been banned and cursed and as practising Muslims, who had already made heavy financial sacrifices to follow the new religion, found no psychological resistance in destroying or throwing away what Allah had forbidden.

In a matter of hours the whole city-state had become abstinent. The most successful campaign that had ever been launched by man against alcohol dependence was miraculously achieved. Can history furnish such example of cheerful submission to the Command of the Master? With one announcement, the use of liquor was prohibited in the society where it had become almost a second nature with a large majority of the people. Not only the Muslims had abstained from the use of intoxicants with this proclamation, but they entertained great fear for what they had practised earlier. Thereupon, Allah told them in the following Verse that they should be careful in future and strictly refrain from its use. Allah would not punish them for its use

15. Quoted by 'Abdullah Ibn 'Umar, Ibn Kathir, op. cit., pp. 640, 641.

in the past. Allah, the Exalted and Majestic, revealed:

لَيْسَ عَلَى الَّذِيْنَ اٰمَنُوْا وَعَمِلُوا الصَّالِحَاتِ جُنَاحٌ فِيْمَا طَعِمُوا إِذَا مَا اتَّقَوْا وَّآمَنُوا وَعَمِلُوا الصّٰلِحَاتِ

"There shall be no sin (imparted) unto those who have believed and done good works for what they may have eaten as long as they fear (Allah) and believe and do good works. (5:93)

While making unlawful the wrong ways of "ignorance", the Holy Qur'an usually ends the instructions with much wholesome words such as : "though what has happened in the past is excepted." It means no action will be taken in regard to those wrong things that one did in ignorance, provided that one mended one's ways and gave up those wrong things in future, after the receipt of a particular Commandment.

Some Commentators of the Holy Qur'an have also alluded to the fifth Verse and given precedence to that over all other Verses dealing with the unlawfulness of drinking wine. The Verse reads thus:

قُلْ إِنَّمَا حَرَّمَ رَبِّيَ الْفَوَاحِشَ مَا ظَهَرَ مِنْهَا وَمَا بَطَنَ وَالإِثْمَ وَالْبَغْيَ بِغَيْرِ الْحَقِّ

"Say: Verily my Lord forbiddeth indecencies, such of them as are apparent and such as are within, and sin and wrongful oppression without any justification." (7:33)

This Verse was revealed in Makkah and sin was declared unlawful in manifest terms and it was demonstrated that drinking wine entailed a great sin (2:219). Here Allah has not defined as to what a sin is, just as silence has been observed in the Divine Word: "And of the fruits of date palm, and grapes whence ye derive strong drink." (16: 67)

Hadrat 'Umar b. al-Khattab (Allah be pleased with him) is reported to have said in one of his Sermons from the pulpit of the Holy

Prophet (peace and blessings of Allah be upon him) :

> "O people, the prohibition of *Khamr* (wine) has been revealed and that is made of five things: Grapes, dates, wheat, barley and honey: and *Khamr* is what covers intellect." *(Bukhari and Muslim)*

Undoubtedly the saying of Caliph 'Umar (Allah be pleased with him) that wine is a drink that covers intellect is an irrefutable explanation and exposition of the reality of wine.

In *Musnad Ahmad, Abu Dawud* and *Tirmidhi*, it is transmitted that Hadrat 'Umar b. al-Khattab (Allah be pleased with him) used to supplicate to Allah like this: "Allah, manifest unto us a sufficient word about wine." When Verse 2: 219 was revealed the Holy Prophet (peace and blessings of Allah be upon him) recited this Verse before 'Umar (Allah be pleased with him) but he continued to pray to Allah to send a decisive word about wine. similar was his reaction on the revelation of the Verse 4:43, but as Verses 5:90, 91 were revealed he was summoned by the Holy Prophet(peace and blessings of Allah be upon him). When the words " Will ye not abstain", appearing in the Verse, arrived Hadrat 'Umar (Allah be pleased with him) exclaimed "We have abstained; we have abstained,"

In this way Allah, The Exalted declared wine unlawful gradually. This process made people to accept the ordinance about the unlawfulness of wine with open heart and keep it at an arm's length. Had wine been declared unlawful in one instance, it would have created hatred against the entire body of *Din* (Islam) in the hearts of the Arabs and drinking wine would have more firmly ingrained in them.

Immediate Submission of the Companions to the Commandment declaring Wine Unlawful

Anas bin Malik (Allah be pleased with him) reported: I was the cup bearer of some people in the house of Abu Talha (Allah be pleased with him) on the day when liquor was forbidden. I was serving a specially prepared strong liquor of fermented date-palm to a group of leading men like Abu Dujana, Abu Ubaida ibn Jarrah, Mu'adh bin Jabal (Allah be pleased with them). As the alcoholic drink started to show its effects on the guests an announcement was heard: "Surely *al-khamr* has been declared unlawful." Anas (Allah be pleased with him) said: "We threw away the remaining liquor in our cups and broke the pots in which other drinks were being fermented." Some of the men performed ablution to purify them selves from a drink they had been guiltlessly taking only a few moments before. Others washed their hole bodies in an act of purification . They perfumed themselves and walked to the Mosque of Madinah to see the Holy Prophet (peace and blessings of Allah be upon him)

Hadrat Anas (Allah be pleased with him) reported: "I was serving people with wine in the house of Abu Talha — and in those days wine was *fadikh* (date-wine) that the Holy Prophet (peace and blessing of Allah be upon him) ordered an announcer to announce : "Lo, verily, Wine has been declared unlawful". On this Abu Talha said: "Come out and spilt it down." "So I went out and poured it down."

(Buhkari)

Hadrat Abu Buraida reported his father saying: As we were sitting around our wine, while we were on a *tillah* and were three or four (companions) and we had jars (of wine) and we used to drink wine lawfully, I stood up till the Holy Prophet (peace and blessings of Allah be upon him) came when the (ordinance of) unlawfulness of wine had been revealed. So I came to my compainions and recited that Commandment to them. They poured down wine from their jars and exclaimed:

"We have abstained, we have abstained."

Hadrat Ibn 'Abbas (Allah be pleased with him) reported that as the Commandment regarding unlawfulness of wine was revealed the Companions went to one another and declared : "Wine has been prohibited and is tantamount to polytheism." *(Tibrani)*

As the Verses 5 : 90, 91 were revealed, these were recited to Hadrat 'Umar (Allah be pleased with him) upto the words "Then will ye (not) shun?" Upon this he said: We have abstained; We have abstained."

From these events you can well imagine the great impact of the Holy Qur'an on the hearts of the believers in the early age of Islam. Allah the Exalted says:

إِنَّمَا الْمُؤْمِنُونَ الَّذِينَ إِذَا ذُكِرَ اللّٰهُ وَجِلَتْ قُلُوبُهُمْ وَإِذَا تُلِيَتْ عَلَيْهِمْ آيَاتُهُ زَادَتْهُمْ إِيمَانًا وَّعَلٰى رَبِّهِمْ يَتَوَكَّلُونَ.

"Verily, the believers are those whose hearts feel fear when Allah is mentioned and when the revelations are recited unto them, they increase their faith, and who trust their Lord." (8:2)

Again Allah Almighty says:

لَوْ أَنْزَلْنَا هٰذَا الْقُرْآنَ عَلٰى جَبَلٍ لَّرَأَيْتَهُ خَاشِعًا مُّتَصَدِّعًا مِّنْ خَشْيَةِ اللّٰهِ وَتِلْكَ الْأَمْثَالُ نَضْرِبُهَا لِلنَّاسِ لَعَلَّهُمْ يَتَفَكَّرُونَ۔

"And had We caused this Qur'an to descend upon a mountain thou (O' Prophet) would have seen it humbled, rent asunder by fear of Allah, such similitudes coin We for mankind that haply they may reflect." (59:21)

Wine is no Cure for diseases but an Ailment

The jurists are at variance among themselves regarding cure by wine, filth and poison. Some jurists have declared it lawful while others have held such a cure as unlawful.

The most correct veiw in this context is that such a cure is permissible under pressing circumstances for in *Bukhari* and *Muslim* we find a Tradition that some people of 'Arina reached

Madinah but the climate of the town did not suit them and their complexion of face turned pale and they suffered flatulence. Upon this the Holy Prophet (peace and blessings of Allah be upon him) advised them to go to the camels of Charity and drink their urine and milk. They went there and drank urine and milk by which they were cured.

The Tradition deals with the compelling circumstance which rendered unlawful food and drink as permissible on the authority of the Qur'anic Verse:

وَقَدْ فَصَّلَ لَكُمْ مَّا حَرَّمَ عَلَيْكُمْ اِلاَّ مَا اضْطُرِرْتُمْ اِلَيْهِ .

> "And He hath expounded unto you what He hath declared unlawful for you save that which you are compelled unto". (6:119)

But cure by wine is discretional as it is drunk to make stomach strong for which their is no authority in the Islamic *Shari'ah*. Cure by wine is, therefore, unlawful because Hadrat Umm Salama (Allah be pleased with her) has reported:

> "My daughter complained to me of sickness. So I prepared *nabidh* for her in an earthen pot. As it was boiling, the Holy Prophet (peace and blessings of Allah be upon him) came to me and asked: "What is this, Umm Salama?" I told him that I cured my daughter by that (*nabidh*). Upon this Allah's Prophet (peace and blessings of Allah be upon him) said: "Allah has not laid the cure of (the diseases of) my *ummah* in things that He has declared unlawful."

Dailama al-Humairi (Allah be pleased with him) reported: I asked the Holy Prophet (peace and blessings of Allah be upon him) about some problem and said: "We live in a cold place and we do hard work there and we prepare wine from wheat, which gives us strength in our works and in the chill of our cities. Upon this the Holy Prophet (peace and blessings of Allah be upon him) said: Does it intoxicate? "Yes", said I. The Holy Prophet (peace and blessings of Allah be upon him) said: Give it up. I said, "people cannot give it up." Upon this the Holy Prophet(peace and blessings of Allah be upon him) remarked: If they do not give it up, then fight with them. *(Abu Dawud)*

Abu Darda' (Allah be pleased with him) reported that the Holy Prophet (peace and blessings of Allah be upon him) said: "Verily, Allah sent down ailment and cure (thereof). So he made a cure for every ailment. So seek cure but seek not cure by unlawful things." *(Abu Dawud)*

Wa'il al-Hadrami (Allah be pleased with him) reported that Tariq b. Suwaid al-Ju'fi (Allah be pleased with him) asked Allah's Messenger (peace and blessings of Allah be upon him) about wine and he forbade (its use) and he expressed hatred that it should be prepared. Al-Ju'fi said, "I prepare it as a medicine, whereupon he (the Holy Prophet) said: It is no medicine, but an ailment. *(Muslim and Abu Dawud)*

Is Wine an Impurity?

In the opinion of the majority of the Jurists wine is a *najasat* (impurity) for Allah, the Exalted has Himself said:

إِنَّمَا الْخَمْرُ وَالْمَيْسِرُ وَالأَنْصَابُ وَالأَزْلاَمُ رِجْسٌ مِنْ عَمَلِ الشَّيْطٰنِ فَاجْتَنِبُوْهُ

"Wine and games of chance, ungodly shrines and divining devices, are abomination of Satan's work; so avoid them." (5:90)

A section of Jurists believes in the cleanliness of wine and take the word *rijs* (abomination) appearing in the Verse for *rijs-ul-Ma'nawi* i. e., abstract abomination for the words "game of chance", "shrines" and "divining devices" and some of these things has at all been qualified with real impurity. Allah, the Exalted says:

فَاجْتَنِبُوا الرِّجْسَ مِنَ الأَوْثَانِ

"Avoid the filth of idols." (22:30)

The word *Authan* (idols) here implies the abstract filth and nobody becomes defile by touching idols for another Verse gives its interpretation that it is a "handiwork of Satan."

In *Subul Al-Salam*,[16] we find that the truth is that the substances in their origin are clean and their unlawfulness does not necessarily imply their impurity. For instance, hemp is unlawful but at the same time it is clean. Contrary to it, impurity (*najasat*) and unlawfulness go hand in hand. Therefore every impure thing is unlawful but every unlawful thing is not impure for law regarding impurity is the prohibition of touching it under all circumstances. Allah has declared garments of silk and gold unlawful for men whereas both the things are not impure. If you have followed the point, the unlawfulness of wine proved by the tenets of the Qur'an and *Ahadith* doest not necessarily imply its impurity.

Rentof Building and Wages of Worker Engaged for Extracting wine are Unlawful

The rent of a building, the wages of a worker, the hiring charges of an animal, a vehicle, a boat or the utensils and the machinery engaged in the production of wine or its sale are totally unlawful and their is no difference of opinion among the Jurists on this point. Allah, the Exalted has in unambiguous terms declared:

يَا اَيُّهَا الَّذِيْنَا اٰمَنُوا اِنَّمَا الْخَمْرُ وَالْمَيْسِرُ وَالْاَنْصَابُ وَالْاَزْلَامُ
رِجْسٌ مِّنْ عَمَلِ الشَّيْطٰنِ فَاجْتَنِبُوْهُ

> "O ye, who believe ! surely, wine and games of chance, (ungodly) shrines and divining devices are abomination of Satan's work; so avoid them. (5:90)

Holy Prophet Mohammad (peace and blessings of Allah be upon him) said:

16. A commentary of the collection of *Hadith* compiled by Ibn Hajr Asqalani and known as *Bulugh ul-Maram*.

Verily, Allah has cursed ten persons: one who squeezes it; one who is engaged for squeezing it; one who drinks it; one who carries it; one to whom it is carried; one who serves drink; one who sells it; one who devours its price; one who purchases it and one for whom it is purchased.

(Ahmad, Ibn Hibban, Tirmidhi, Abu Dawud and Ibn Maja)

Again, Allah, the Exalted has said:

وَذَرُوْا ظَاهِرَ الِاثْمِ وَبَاطِنَهُ ط

"And forsake the outwardness of sin and the inwardness thereof," (6:120)

وَلاَ تَعَاوَنُوا عَلَى الاِثْمِ

"And help not one another unto sin." (5:2)

Some Strange Stories about Drunkards

Hadrat 'Uthman (Allah be pleased with him), the third Caliph of Islam, delivered a sermon upon the pulpit of the Holy Prophet (peace and blessings of Allah be upon him) and said:

"Avoid wine for it is the fountainhead of evils. There lived a man before you who had devoted himself to worship and withdrew himself from people. A dissolute woman came to live with him. He sent his slave-girl to bring him some information about her. He entered the room with her and as he entered the door the slave-girl shut it till he reached another beautiful woman who had a boy and a mug of wine. She said: "By Allah, I have not invited you to divulge any information. Instead, I have invited you to have illicit relation with me or to kill this boy or to drink this mug of wine. He took a mug of wine and said: "Give me more wine." Thus he continued to drink till he committed fornication with her and murdered the boy. So shun wine for wine and Faith never go hand in hand but either of the two hastens to expel the other." (*Baihaqi*)

Ibn Abi Dunya says:

> "I saw a drunkard in some street of Baghdad. He was drinking urine and wiping his face with his urine and was saying: "Our Allah, make me of repentants and make me one of the righteous."

Hadrat 'Abdur Rahman prepared some food and wine and invited some Companions of the Holy Prophet (peace and blessings of Allah be upon him) when drinking wine was not yet banned. They ate and drank till they were intoxicated and the time of sun-set prayer became due. One of the Companions left for prayer and he recited *Sura* The disbelievers" (*al-Kafirin*) wrongly as thus: "Say: O' disbelievers, I worship not that which ye worship and we worship that which ye worship."

The history is replete with hundreds of strange stories about drunkards that are sufficient enough to exhort every body having faith in religion and endowed with wisdom and manliness to avoid wine and other intoxicants. Allah, our Great Master, is true in saying: "Verily, it (wine) is an abomination of Satan's work: so avoid it that ye may prosper." (5:91). The Holy Prophet (peace and blessings of Allah be upon him) also termed wine as "a fountainhead of evils."

We should, therefore, raise our hands before Allah and make humble supplication to Him: Our Allah, bestow upon us Thy fear that is a barrier between us and Thy disobedience and bestow upon us to be Thy obedient that should lead us to Thy Paradise and enrich us in Faith that should make the calamities of the word weight upon us."

"Our Allah! have mercy on us in forsaking sins as long as we live; and have mercy on us lest we should undertake some painful tasks that are not beneficial to us; and bestow on us an excellent look that pleaseth Thee. Our Lord, take us not to task if we forget or commit error. Our Lord, impose not on us that which we have not the power to bear; pardon us, absolve us and have mercy on us. Thou art our Protector, grant us victory over the disbelieving folk."

"Our Allah, let our religion suit us for the chastity of our work; and let our world suit us, in which lies our livelihood and let our Hereafter suit us wherein is our Next world; and let (our span of life) prolong in every good; and let our death be a relief for us from all evils."

CHAPTER 4

The True Motive in the Prohibition of Khamr

The real motivation in the success of prohibition of *Khamr* (intoxicants) came from Islam as a religion and a way of life. The Qur'anic Verses which deal directly with the problem of intoxication, as we have seen, include clear elements of "persuasion" and "incentive manipulation." However, the real moving force for this campaign had started many years before. The prohibition of *Khamr* did not take only three years to achieve as some modern scholars have asserted. It had actually commenced thirteen years before when the rising sun of Islam sent its first blessed rays to illuminate the dark valley and mountains of Makkah.

Instead of initially prohibiting alcohol intoxication and other pre- -Islamic Arabs customs and traditions, Islam first attacked the deep-rooted false beliefs and values upon which they were based. Idolatry, triblalism and the values of the ancient Arab moarlity were the real source of 'ignorance' (*Jahiliyyah*) as the Holy Qur'an calls it. These were the real sources of the evils of which gambling, adultery, and alcoholism were simply symptoms; they were only fruits of the tree of *Jahiliyyah* the main root of which was idolatry.

That is why Islam spent the first thirteen years of its life devoting itself to establishing the new faith in its converts. Faith in the One Almighty Allah, in the Hereafter with its Paradise and Hell, in the

Unseen Angels and in the Prophets (peace be upon them) and the revealed Holy Books.

That was not an easy task. When the ancient Arab fully accepted the new faith he would never be the same man again. It was transformation from prostrating himself to the stone-carved god of his tribe, which was supposed to give him support against other Arab tribes and to Justify all his immoral acts like robbing and looting others, killing his female children, gambling, intoxicating himself and fornicating freely. Now he listened to the Holy Qur'an to converse him with his true Creator, to All-Knowing Mighty Allah:

وَلَقَدْ خَلَقْنَا الإنْسَانَ وَنَعْلَمُ مَا تُوَسْوِسُ بِهِ نَفْسُهُ وَنَحْنُ اَقْرَبُ اِلَيْهِ مِنْ حَبْلِ الْوَرِيْدِ

"We verily created a man and We know what his soul whispereth to him, and we are nearer to him than his jugular vein."(50:16)

وَعِنْدَهُ مَفَاتِحُ الْغَيْبِ لاَ يَعْلَمُهَا اِلاَّهُوَ ط وَيَعْلَمُ مَا فِى الْبَرِّ وَالْبَحْرِ ط وَمَا تَسْقُطُ مِنْ وَّرَقَةٍ اِلاَّ يَعْلَمُهَا وَلاَ حَبَّةٍ فِى ظُلُمٰتِ الاَرْضِ وَلاَ رَطْبٍ وَّلاَ يَابِسٍ اِلاَّفِى كِتٰبٍ مُبِيْنٍ.

"And with Him are the keys of the invisible. None but He knoweth them. And He knoweth what is in the land and in the sea. Not a leaf falleth but He knoweth it, not a grain amid the darkness of the earth, naught of wet or dry but (it is noted) in a clear record." (6:59)

It is not the dead god of a tribe, nor even a god of all Arabs, but He is the Allah of all mankind, of the Heavens and the earth, of the seen and the unseen. No more narrow selfish tribalistic pride since Allah is the Merciful Compassionate Sustainer of all men. The only norm for better and worse among people is belief in Allah and good deeds to mankind. The Holy Qur'an says:

يَا اَيُّهَا النَّاسُ اِنَّا خَلَقْنَاكُمْ مِنْ ذَكَرٍ وَّاُنْثٰى وَجَعَلْنَاكُمْ شُعُوْباً وَّقَبَائِلَ لِتَعَارَفُوْا ط اِنَّ اَكْرَمَكُمْ عِنْدَاللّٰهِ اَتْقٰكُمْ ط اِنَّ اللّٰهَ عَلِيْمٌ خَبِيْرٌ.

"O' mankind! Lo! we have created you male and female, and have made you nations and tribes that ye may know one another. Lo! the noblest of you, in the sight of Allah, is the best in conduct. Lo! Allah is Knower, Aware." (49:13)

The Holy Prophet (peace and blessings of Allah be upon him) supported these Qur'anic Verses by his famous *Hadith* in which he clearly stated that people are as equal as the "teeth of a comb." That there is no preference for an Arab over a non-Arab except through better conduct and fear of Allah.

Compare this new attitude of international all-embracing humaneness portrayed by this Qur'anic Verse and the extreme, proud, fanatical tribalism of pre-Islamic Arabia which the great poet repeated:

"And when a newborn in our tribe,
reaches the age of weaning,
Tyrants prostrate themselves to him,
in submission and yielding."

The distance between the two stands was long and arduous, but the Muslims were able to bridge this gap through severe bodily and psychic sufferings at the hands of the tribal chiefs of Makkah. Suhayb, the Roman; Bilal, the Abyssinian; and Salman, the Persian, who had been among those pioneers later became exalted leaders of the new state of Madinah in spite of the fact that they were non-Arab.

For thirteen years in Makkah the Holy Qur'an had been hammering on the realities of the Hereafter and of Resurrection, so that the fear of punishment in Hell and the eternal rewards in Paradise became vivid realities to the Muslims. The Holy Qur'an says:

إِذَا السَّمَاءُ انْفَطَرَتْ. وَإِذَا الْكَوَاكِبُ انْتَثَرَتْ. وَإِذَا الْبِحَارُ فُجِّرَتْ. وَإِذَا الْقُبُوْرُ بُعْثِرَتْ. عَلِمَتْ نَفْسٌ مَّا قَدَّمَتْ وَأَخَّرَتْ.

"When the heaven is cleft asunder. When the planets are dispersed.

When the seas are poured forth. And the sculptures are overturned. A soul will know what it hath sent before (it) and what left behind? (82:1-5)

After the Muslim Arabs abandoned idolatry and the tribalism the tree of pre-Islamic morality lost its roots and the social customs of alcoholism, gambling and adultery were now like weak branches in a dying tree. Or better still, like neurotic symptoms which continued to have some form of functional autonomy long after their inner conflicts and complexes had been resolved. A simple course of symptomatic behavioural therapy will remove them without any chances for future symptom substitution. The task of prohibition *Khamr* was also made easier because during these long years Islam had dealt with many of the more serious problems which brought insecurity to the Arab family.

The murder of female children was not only prohibited but Arabs were even bitterly criticized by the Holy Qur'an for being ashamed of having female babies. Some of the Qur'anic Verses vividly exemplified this criminal act in a quick sequence of the horrors of the Hereafter. The Holy Qur'an says:

وَإِذَا الْوُحُوْشُ حُشِرَتْ. وَإِذَا الْبِحَارُ سُجِّرَتْ. وَإِذَا النُّفُوْسُ
زُوِّجَتْ. وَإِذَا الْمَوْءُدَةُ سُئِلَتْ. بِاَيِّ ذَنْبٍ قُتِلَتْ.

"And when the wild beasts are herded together; and when the seas rise; and when souls are reunited; and when the girl-child that was buried alive asked for what sin she was slain?" (81:5-9)

Again the Holy Qur'an says:

وَإِذَا بُشِّرَ اَحَدُهُمْ بِالْاُنْثٰى ظَلَّ وَجْهُهٗ مُسْوَدًّا وَّهُوَ كَظِيْمٌ.
يَتَوَارٰى مِنَ الْقَوْمِ مِنْ سُوْءِ مَا بُشِّرَ بِهٖ ط اَيُمْسِكُهٗ عَلٰى هُوْنٍ
اَمْ يَدُسُّهٗ فِى التُّرَابِ ط اَلَا سَاءَ مَا يَحْكُمُوْنَ.

"When if one of them receiveth tidings of the birth of a female, his face remaineth darkened, and he is wrath inwardly. He hideth himself from the folk because of the evil of that whereof he hath had tidings, (asking himself): shall he keep it in contempt, or bury it beneath the dust. Verily evil is their judgment." (16:58,59)

Many other evils concerning women and family structure and functions were also abolished e.g., women were given inheritance, they were allowed to choose their husbands and that matter of inheriting the wives of one's deceased father was strictly prohibited. The Holy Qur'an says:

وَلاَ تَنْكِحُوا مَا نَكَحَ آبَاؤُكُمْ مِنَ النِّسَاءِ إِلاَّ مَا قَدْ سَلَفَ ط إِنَّهُ
كَانَ فَاحِشَةً وَّمَقْتًا ط وَسَاءَ سَبِيْلاً .

"And marry not those women whom your fathers married, except what hath already happened (of that nature) in the past. Lo! it was ever lewdness and abomination, and an evil way." (4:22)

In short, for those psychologists who look at the family as the main source of developing insecure future alcoholics, what Islam did in this field will be for great interest. It is a field greatly neglected by Muslim psychologists.

Muslim children in Madinah were given much greater love and effection. The Holy Prophet(peace and blessings of Allah be upon him) as the living example of Islam used to lead the prayer while carrying his beloved baby grand-daughter. His older grandson would ride on his blessed back while he was in prostration posture himself in congregational prayer. He would continue in this position until the boy finished his play, thus causing all those who prayed behind him to wonder about the long time he took in prostration.

The new feelings of peace and security in the Muslim family and the acquired sense of pride that women had must have helped to ease the problems of the 'drying' alcoholics.

Also children who grew in these families were less likely to develop the extreme emotional insecurity which was over compensated by the false tribal pride of ancient Arabs.

It is important to mention at this stage that what has been stated above with regard to the efforts of Islam in laying the foundation of faith before attacking the evil social Arab custom has already been clearly exemplified by Hadrat 'A' isha (Allah be pleased with her) the wife of Prophet Muhammad (peace and blessings of Allah be upon him) some time after his death. Without the modern jargon of the social sciences Hadrat 'A'isha (Allah be pleased with her) simply said that if the Holy Qur'an first told the Arabs not to drink *Khamr* and to stop being adulterous they would have said, "No, we will never comply" ; but the Holy Qur'an kept putting in their hearts the fear of Allah and of Hell until they were softened. Then they were commanded to discontinue these acts and they complied."

CHAPTER 5

Evil Effects of Drinking Wine and other Intoxicants

There are manifold reasons for prohibition of intoxicating liquor. Drinking is a serious crime. Drunkenness often leads to the loss of senses which is responsible for commission of various anti-social crimes. Drunkenness is extremely harmful, as it kills man's capacity to distinguish between right and wrong, good and evil, virtue and vice. A Drunkard in his intoxication performs such acts which result in enmity and hatred and which disturbs the peace and tranquillity of family and society. Drinking not only destroys man's health but also his wealth, and kills his sense of dignity. Thus wine is injurious both from temporal and spiritual points of view:

1. Temporal

(a) Intellectual

The most precious gift of Allah to mankind is the intellect. It is because of his reasoning power that man is called the best creation of Allah.

Intellect has two very strong enemies: Desire and Anger. These two rivals of intellect get reinforcement by alcoholic liquor. When alcoholic liquor enters the human body the first victim is the highest cerebral centres which control such factors as judgment, sense of responsibility and moral integrity. When these higher factors are depressed, the Lower instincts are released from captivity. Moral and social inhibitions become a dead thing. It is now proved that the intoxicated person becomes talkative, excited or even violent and aggressive. On-lookers think that he is stimulated. In fact it is not stimulation. What is often refered to as alcoholic stimulation is the first sign of alcoholic depression. No amount of alcohol can stimulate intellectual functions.

Wine covers intellect and power of discerning right from wrong. There is no act which a man cannot do when he loses his sense and wisdom. This temporary covering over the intellectual region has got necessary repercussion on mind which can produce many diseases hitherto unknown to a drunkard.

Wine weakens the faculty of understanding and its overall effect on the whole nervous system mostly makes the drunkard a victim to insanity and degenerates him to a vindictive beast. Sirajuddin 'Umar b. Alwardi has explained this reality as under:

"Give up wine if thou art brave,
How can one indulge in an act of insanity,
Who hath understanding."

Wine also causes delirium — a disease that destroys the memory of a drunkard. Wine provokes indignation because a drunkard is infuriated on petty grounds. Wine induces the alcoholics to frequent treachery. It excites some drunkards to sudden weeping, some to savagious contraction, some to unbounded liveliness and still some others to extreme humiliation and disgrace. Whims and caprices also haunt the mind of the alcoholic and "he loseth both the world and the Hereafter. That is the loss manifest." (22:11)

(b) Physical

There are a number of physical conditions associated with alcoholism. The main ones are:

1. *Alcohol Intoxication* : Mild to moderate intoxication can produce gastric irritation and vomiting. It can produce "behavioural changes," such as depression or aggressiveness. It can bring on alcoholic stupor. Another well-known result of alcohol intoxication is the "hangover" or "mourning after". It is possible, through too much digestion of alcohol at one time, to induce a "coma" — a true emergency from which death may result

2. *Inson nia or Nightmares*: When the alcoholic can sleep, he often has terrible nightmares. Often he cannot sleep and constantly he craves for a drink.

3. *Convulsive Seizures*: These "fits" sometimes occur in clusters and not always when the individual is drinking. Alcohol, not epilepsy, is probably the greatest single cause of convulsions.

4. *Alcoholic Hallucination*: In this instance the individual has moved, at least temporarily, out of the real world and into a complete fantasy world. He may even hold conversations with an invisible partner. Alcohol makes the brain so irritable that it sees, hears and feels things that are not there.

5. *Delirium Tremens*: Delirium tremens occur when an alcoholic is deprived of liquor. They are accompanied by deep confusion and disorientation. He is unable to stop moving. He paces around, tears at his bed linen, has terrifying hallucinations. He is obsessed with terror. In a small percentage of cases even death may result. Delirium tremens are considered a medical emergency. Immediate hospitalization is necessary. the treatment consists of comprehensive physical evaluation by a doctor, constant nursing, adequate sedation, maintenance of fluid in the body and addition of vitamin supplements.

DISEASES OF THE ALCOHOLIC

Conditions such as these are not yet the worst of it for the alcoholic. There are also chronic disorders due to prolonged usage of alcohol. Some of the more common ones are:

1. *Neurological Disorders*: These are associated with marked, permanent and irreversible disabilities of the nerves. They leave a lasting imprint upon intellect, emotional balance, motor and sensory control. Continued exposure to alcohol can lead to the accumulated destruction of brain cells.

2. *Digestive Disorders*: Nausea, diarrhoea and vomiting are merely the beginning of alcoholism. Eventually severe ulcers and hemorrhaging may result.

3. *Liver Ailments*: An acute enlargement of the liver may appear within several days of heavy drinking. Liver diseases—the most prominent of which *Cirrhosis*—are very dangerous. Non-drinkers may also contract *Cirrhosis*. However, the incidence is eight times higher among heavy drinkers. The exact pathology is not known. In some way alcohol, when coupled with dietary (vitamin) deficiencies, seems instrumental in causing the hardening and shrinking of the liver. This prevents its normal functioning and may lead to death.

   Cirrhosis is often a permanent and serious condition. It first affects the individual in term of weakness ad fatigue. In more advanced cases the liver is likely to become harder and smaller. There are disturbances in clotting mechanisms. Retained fluids sometimes cause serious problems. Death may result from a number of causes ones the liver is weakened.

4. *Pancreatitis*: This is usually dismissed as gastritis in its mildest form. On the other hand, in alcoholics trouble with the pancreas may be an acute abdominal emergency. In this severe form dangerous hemorrhaging may occur.

5. *Nutritional Deficiency and Cardiac Diseases*: *Pellagra* and various anemias may result from alcoholism. So, too, many respiratory conditions and heart abnormalities. There is some evidence that alcohol constricts the arteries of the heart. Recent studies suggest that alcohol taken in great quantity, can injure the heart muscle. By causing considerable change in the circulation of the blood, it overtaxes the heart and increases its workload.

6. *Oral Cancer*: Alcohol and smoking are fingered by some as being the chief culprits for bringing about the changes associated with oral cancer. The American Dental Association lists the following oral changes that are symptomatic of cancer:

(a) swelling of the palate or other area within the mouth;

(b) Persistent red spots, particularly on the floor of the mouth;

(c) White patches on oral tissues;

(d) Ulceration (s) of the lip or in the mouth;

(e) redness of the oral mucosa with accompanying burning sensations.

7. *Diabetes*: Though alcohol does not appear to cause or contribute to the advent of diabetes, it may aggravate the condition of the diabetic by increasing the sugar count in the blood to a dangerous degree or by lowering the sugar level of the blood dangerously, or by preventing sugar from the liver to enter the blood when needed to maintain proper sugar levels. This is likely to happen when drinking "on-an-empty-stomach," as when before-dinner cocktails are taken.

There diseases and their complications often result in disability and death. the sort of life many alcoholics who persist in drinking are forced to lead is often a "fate worse then death." It is a life devoid of meaningful adult relationship, with no real happiness or opportunity for gratification.

Drinking wine weakens the coming generation; the child of an alcoholic is often weak and the descendants of the drunkard's son are even weaker, physically and intellectually. In this way weakness is transmitted to generation after generation till the drunkard's posterity is extinct, specially, when the descendants follow the example of their forefathers.

Drinking wine also causes euphorbia. Some German doctors say that the texture of a young drunkard of forty years is like the texture of the body of a seventy years old man who does not drink wine.

Wine consumption causes frequent abortions, increases the ratio of death of children of those mothers who are addicted to wine. The reports of the U.N.O. bear evidence to the fact that people addicted to wine are short-aged than other people. Dr. Charles Richet says that the alcoholics have left no room in the hospitals and lunatic asylums in France.[1] The assertion of a European doctor also reinforces this statement. He says, "Look up half of the wine-shops and i guarantee you against half of the hospitals."

(c) Economic

It is also a veritable evil from economic point of view, as it forms a chief source of the drainage of money from the coffers of a drunkard. The Holy Qur'an deprecates this unnecessary drainage of money by saying:

اِنَّ الْمُبَذِّرِيْنَ كَانُوْا اِخْوَانَ الشَّيَاطِيْنِ ط

"Verily those who spend extravagantly are the brothers of the devils." (17:27)

Drinking wine destroys wealth and dilapidates property: especially, in these days when wine is of numerous kinds according to the degree of its intoxication and when its price is soaring high. The merchants of wine are seduced to adopt illegal and unfair means to promote drinking among people. Some people simultaneously carry on the business of fornication, immodesty and corruption and other ways of luxuriant living in order to attract alcoholics to wine just as some people introduce gambling of various kinds along with drinking. A man enters a casino with thousands of pounds in his pocket but comes out of it penniless with the loss of wit and health.

We seek refuge in Allah against the covetous people and their devilish mischiefs. "Such are they who have lost their souls and that which they used to invent hath failed them." (11:21)

1. Alcohol, p. 116.

(d) Psychological Harms

1. The drunkards are prone to divulge secrets — a very dangerous feature associated with drinking; particularly when alcoholics have intimate contacts with the Government and politicians of the countries or chiefs of the armed forces, the police or Defence departments. The foreign agents always depend upon wine to ensure the success of their important mission for which they are deputed.

2. The alcoholic becomes a slave of wine because he can hardly give it up. Wine has penetrating effect on all humàn nerves which off and on urge man to drink wine and thus he indulges in lavish drinking. But all this does not serve as a warning to him with the ultimate result that he is condemend to obscurity and languidness. When an alcoholic recovers his senses, he finds himself helpless to leave the habit of drinking wine. His inclination to drinking becomes stronger and therefore, he is unable to get rid of it.

3. Drinking wine extinguishes noble passions of mercy, sympathy and tenderness. We should seek refuge in Allah against the mischief of the covetous and the misled. "Lo! that is the loss manifest." (22:11).

(e) Social Harms

1. Factions, quarrels and disputes of various types emerge out on account of wine among the alcoholics themselves on the one hand and among the alcoholics and other people on the other hand, simply because an alcoholic falls in to a fit of passion. Allah, the Eternal says:

إِنَّمَا يُرِيدُ الشَّيْطٰنُ اَنْ يُّوقِعَ بَيْنَكُمُ الْعَدَاوَةَ وَالْبَغْضَاءَ فِى الْخَمْرِ وَالْمَيْسِرِ

"Only would satan sow hatred and strife among you, by wine, and games of chance." (5:91)

2. Drinking wine causes lowliness and disgrace in the sight of people. The alcoholic becomes a laughing stock due to his funny talks, actions and behaviour. People scoff at him and children sport with him as he behaves like an idiot. We find a number of strange actions and parables about the alcoholics that are sufficient for every noble, wise and manly person to abstain from drinking wine.

3. The drunkard ventures to commit the most heinous offences of murder and fornication, disgraces people and defies the law and canons of society.

4. Drinking wine is extremely dangerous for the passengers of ships and aeroplanes, the drivers of trains and buses and for the pilots of aeroplanes.

The statistics of accidents bear an ample testimony to the fact that more than 30 per cent accidents are the results of drinking wine and on this account wine has been characterized as a fountainhead of evils (*umm-ul-khaba'ith*), an embodiment of sins (*majma'ul-atham*), a door to mischief (*miftah-ush-sharr*), culmination of all lewdness and the most abominable act of all major sins.

We seek refuge in Allah against the mischiefs of our soul and against our evil deeds.

2. Spiritual

1. Wine is the mother of all sins. There is no sin which an alcoholic cannot commit when he loses his intellect. An alcoholic loses his power of control and self- restraint and lets loose the god of Cupid to satisfy his sexual lust. This is extremely harmful for the elevation of soul to spiritual heights.

2. Drinking wine extinguishes the glow of faith. This point is elaborated at lenght in a Tradition of the Holy Prophet (peace and blessings of Allah be upon him) that embodies the maxim:

وَلاَ يَشْرَبُ الْخَمْرَ حِيْنَ يَشْرَبُهَا وَهُوَ مُؤْمِنٌ

"And a person, at the time of drinking wine is not a believer."
(Bukhari)

This Tradition deals with a bold fact that a person who relishes the odour of faith can never think of drinking wine. In other words a person who drinks wine is devoid even an iota of faith at the time of drinking.

According to another Tradition transmitted by *Hakim,* a renowned scholar of Tradition, on the authority of Abu Huraira (Allah be pleased with him) the Holy Prophet (peace and blessings of Allah be upon him) said: "whosoever" commits fornication or drinks wine, Allah deprives him of faith just as a man takes off his shirt from over his head."

3. It keeps a man away from the remembrance of Allah , which is the object of man's creation in this world. The drunkards cannot even say their prayer correctly, especially the *Salat* (prayer) which is the fundamental pillar of Islam. The Holy Qur'an says:

وَيَصُدَّكُمْ عَنْ ذِكْرِ اللّٰهِ وَعَنِ الصَّلٰوةِ فَهَلْ اَنْتُمْ مُنْتَهُوْنَ.

"And (wine) turn you aside from the remembrance of Allah, and from prayer; Will you not, therefore, abstain from them?"(5:91)

When this Verse was recited to Hadrat 'Umar b. al-Khattab (Allah be pleased with him), the Second Caliph of Islam, he said "We have abstained; we have abstained."

Nothing is more detrimental and deceitful for a Muslim than an act which turns him aside from the remembrance of Allah and observance of His Commands and disturbs his communion with his Creator. An addict of intoxicants spoils his health, ruins his wealth and property, distracts his soul from the remembrance of Allah and prayer and becomes loathsome in the eyes of public masses.

4. There is no denying the fact that evil effects of wine are not confined to human body. Drinking affects the morals of man as well as the effect is most pernicious. It no less contributes to the incitement of enmity and hatred among the fellow beings which are bad both from temporal and spiritual points of view.

We seek refuge in Allah against wine and its sister evils and say:

Say unto him who drinketh wine inadvertently:
Thou liveth due to wine an abominable life;
The value of man lies in his wit;
Why, then, O' brother of ignorance,
Thou hath sold that for a lowly thing?
O' resolute brother, give it up immediately;
It is an embodiment of all evil habits;
It is a door to all evils and harms,
Lock up the door, live not in trouble.

An anti-alcohol organisation was founded in America in 1874 A.D. after an attack of alcoholism on the Middle West. This organisation has its branches in some Arab countries as well and it disseminates its teaching against drinking and wine trading. In some Islamic states like the Kingdom of Saudi Arabia and Arab Republic of Libya wine is totally prohibited. Other Islamic states should also follow suit and ban wine without further loss of time. What are they waiting for in declaring wine unlawful?

أَلَمْ يَأْنِ لِلَّذِيْنَ اٰمَنُوْا اَنْ تَخْشَعَ قُلُوْبُهُمْ لِذِكْرِ اللّٰهِ وَمَا نَزَلَ
مِنَ الحَقِّ وَلاَ يَكُونُوْا كَالَّذِيْنَ اُوتُوا الْكِتَابَ مِنْ قَبْلُ فَطَالَ
عَلَيْهِمُ الْاَمَدُ فَقَسَتْ قُلُوْبُهُمْ ط وَكَثِيْرٌ مِّنْهُمْ فَاسِقُوْنَ.

"Is not the time ripe for the hearts of those who believe to submit to Allah's reminder and to the Truth which is revealed, that they become not as those who received the Scripture of old but the term was prolonged for them and so their hearts were hardened, and many of them are evil-lovers." (57:16)

Again the Holy Qur'an says:

وَلَقَدْ يَسَّرْنَا الْقُرْاٰنَ لِلذِّكْرِ فَهَلْ مِنْ مُّدَّكِرٍ.

"And in truth We have made the Qur'an easy to remember;[2] but is there any that remembereth." (54:17)

It is obligatory on all Islamic countries to declare wine and promulgate its prohibition in the cities to enforce the Divine limits (*hudud*) for "whosoever transgresseth Allah's limits, such are wrong-doers." (2:229)

Paltry Benefits of Wine

There are some benefits of wine but they are quite insignificant and negligible as compared with the tremendous harms, grievous afflictions and dangerous calamities that wine entails. Some of these paltry benefits are as under:

1. People deal in wine because it is a great source of wealth in some countries.
2. It is contended that wine provides a cure for some diseases but wine is just like various poisons and dangerous vegetables having moderate propensities. This contention is altogether wrong. The medical science has proved that wine is of no avail in curing diseases and theory of medical treatment by wine is totally incorrect. Contrary to it, everybody who probes into the

2. It is a fact that the Qur'an is marvellously easy for believers to commit to memory. Thousands of people in the East know the whole book by heart. The translator, who find great difficulty in remembering well-known quotations, accurately can remember page after page of the Qur'an in Arabic with perfect accuracy (Marmaduke pickthall, *The Meaning of the Glorious Qur'an*, p. 793).

books on medicines will be astonished to note that wine plavs a major part to cause different diseases.

3. Wine is supposed to provide consolation to a meloncholy person against the aftermath of an action that multiplies grief and sorrow.

4. Wine causes excessive discharge of urine. Thus the excessiveness of wine is sometimes attributable to the fluidity of alcohol. Even the limpid water, when taken in excessive quantity, also excites discharge of urine. This is not useful because it damages other organs of human body. Further diuretics are fond as long as man suffers from some diseases of the urinary organs. Therefore diuretics keep security and do not entail fatal harms which alcohol contains.

5. Wine is an impetus to valour and arrogance which are considered as great benefits of wine by the Arab and Bedouins. In this modern age it is held very dangerous as the enthusiasm excited by wine sow enmity and hatred among the drunkards. This enthusiasm is no longer required in the modern warfare because war has become a very intricate technique these days which warrants brisk wit and sharp insight of which the alcoholics are devoid of. A miser becomes, in a state of intoxication, generous and a stingy becomes a spendthrift. This behaviour of an alcoholic proved beneficial in the past when an alcoholic, under intoxication, would spend his money among his family. But in these days this behaviour of a drunkard is full of dangers because he spends his money among people out side his family, rather he promotes wide sale and circulation of wine among his shameless companions free of charge. Such are the insignificant and negligible benefits of wine.

We seek refuge in Allah against wine and its sister evils and against the worship of evil promptings of the Satan.

CHAPTER 6

Some Expert Opinions about Alcohol and Modern Researches on Alcoholism

Some Expert Opinions about Alcohol

Dr. Abdul Wahhab says:

"When we approach the Scholars of religion, Doctors of medicines, Ethologists, sociologists and Economists and seek their opinion about wine, they are unanimous in their experession about its evil effect on human life. They strongly prohibit wine."

The Scholars of religion say:

It is unlawful, for ,all evil stem out of it."

The Doctors Opine:

"Wine is one of the greatest dangers menacing humanity not only because of its poisonous harms directly affecting the alcoholic but also for its unhealthy aftermaths. When it is a road to danger, its harms are not meagre — the very dreadful harm is tuberculosis. Wine weakens the body and reduces the power of resistance against various diseases. It adversely affects all the organs of human body particularly lever and tremendously weakens the entire nervous system. It is one of the main causes of nerve diseases and a factor leading to madness, villainy and crimes not only on the part of his coming posterity. Thus wine is a fountainhead of mis-fortune, distitution and adversity and the genesis of poverty, wretchedness and humiliation."

The Ethologists say:

> "In order to safeguard sedateness, chastity, nobility, pride and manliness, it is essential for a man to abstain from eating such things as disarm him of these salient traits of character."

The Social Reformers say:

> "In order to maintain complete law and order in the society, it is essential to avoid all inclinations towards such activities as disturb the social order and cause chaos to reign for chaos creates dissensions which serve the interest of the enemy."

An eminent Sociologist, Dr. Seldon D. Bacon at Yales School of Alcohol Studies states:

> "Alcoholism affects with shock, disgust or fright and costs the individual heart-ache, money and strength."[1]

The Economists says:

> "Every pound that we spend for our benefit provides strength to us and our country whereas every pound that we spend without any benefit is a loss to us and our country. What is, then, the position of millions of pounds that go in waste on drinking wine of various kinds resulting into our retrogression in the economic field and deprivation of manliness and national pride?"

Allah, the Exalted says:

وَلاَ تُفْسِدُوْا فِي الْاَرْضِ بَعْدَ اِصْلاَ حِهَا ط ذَالِكُمْ خَيْرٌ لَّكُمْ اِنْ كُنْتُمْ مُؤْمِنِيْنَ.

> "And work not corruption on the earth after fair ordering thereof. That is better for you if ye are believers." (7:85)

أَمْ حَسِبَ الَّذِيْنَ اجْتَرَحُوا السَّيِّئَاتِ اَنْ نَجْعَلَهُمْ كَالَّذِيْنَ اٰمَنُوا وَعَمِلُوا الصَّالِحَاتِ سَوَاءً مَّحْيَاهُمْ وَمَمَاتُهُمْ سَاءَ مَا يَحْكُمُوْنَ.

> "Or do those who commit evil deeds suppose that We shall make

1. *Mujallah al-Tamaddun.i-Islami* quoted from *fiqh al-Sunnah* by Syed Sabih, Vol. II, p. 372.

them as those who believe and do good work (and make) their life and death equal? Bad is their judgment." (45:21)

Modern Researches on Alcohol and its Action on the Human Organism

Modern scientific research shows that the use of liquor has numerous undesirable effects on human life. It upsets proper functioning of the body, the power of reasoning, the balance of mind and the structure of society. Suicide, homicide, crime and insanity get great stimulus from this abominable habit. Drunkenness gives rise to impulses which are greatly anti-social. The tragedy of alcoholism is that the alcoholic cannot discard this habit because alcohol destroys the greater part of his reason and self-control. The modern scientists, after carrying on a long research on alcohol, clearly say that alcohol is the mother of all evils.

The credit for exploding the old, long established theory about wine is due to Mr. Krepelin, a psychologist, who has, with the support of some other psychologists, shown that even a single doze of the smallest quantity of wine does harm to the microbes in the human brain and impairs the finest sensitive centres. Similarly, Mr. Hodge has made some experiments with regard to the effects of alcohol on the muscles and he has come to the conclusion that the use of wine injures the power of endurance and patience, and dulls one's keenness. Mr. Alexander Brice, an expert in dietetics, expresses his considered opinion about wine in the following words:

> "There can no longer be any doubt that it is in reality a tissue poison of the first order which manifests its narcotising and finally degenerative action chiefly on the nervous system. It has indeed no claim to be termed a stimulant, being in plain terms, only a drug with a temporary exhilarating effect followed thereafter by a long period of depression. The conclusion of practically all thoughtful medical men is that it is quite unnecessary to health, and if not of

doubtful value in the treatment of disease, is at least capable of being replaced in most instances by less dangerous substances."

When these researches opened the eyes of the people of understanding, persons of other professions also turned their attention to this subject. For instance, Sir Frederick Treves, speaking of the troops who had been sent to raise the siege of Lady Smith in the Boer War, said in his report:

> "In that enormous column of 20,000 men the first who dropped were not the tall men, or the short men or the big men or the little men — they were the drinkers, and they dropped out as clearly as if they had been labelled with a big letter on their back."

Walker and Freuod have found that rats given nutritious diet with alcohol for a period of five months, and then taken off alcohol for a period of thirty years, obtained comparatively poor scores in learning and recent memory tests in relation to non-alcohol-imbibing control rats.[2] After carrying out a number of researches with human objects, Dr. Noble concluded that prolonged drinking of alcohol, even in small quantities, is implicated in permanent damage to memory and learning ability.[3]

It is not merely in the physical sphere that alcohol works such havoc, but its destructiveness extends to the most finely developed part of the human being, personality and his morals, owing to the fact that it affects first and foremost the higher function of the brain which determines ethical concepts even before it affects that part which determines physical action. The people who are in the habit of using intoxicants sometimes appear to have no sense of shame and evince a lack of responsibility to others. Alcohol also affects badly the female's personality. According to Charle E. Ramsgate of New York City, she becomes a spitting and slovenly animal incapable of

2. Arthur Fisher, "*Danger: Social Drinking*, recent experiments prove that it can cost more than you realize," *Reader's Digest*, July, 1976 issue.

3. *Ibid.*

anything but the sordid — a disgrace to herself, to her sex and society. William McDougall, the eminent British Psychologist, says:

> "If you take a pe-son of the inexpressive temperament, one who has an extreme example, who stands at the very bottom of the scale of readiness of emotional expression and administer to him successive small doses of ethyl alcohol, you push him step by step about the scale of expressiveness until when he has absorbed into his blood a reasonable large dose, he is ready to fall on your neck at the slightest provocation and to weep or love or laugh or rage or display himself and assert his powers and opinions with the utmost freedom, a total absence of his usual reserve. These facts are no new discoveries to the laboratory. They were known to the ancients, but it seems to have been reserved to themselves to point out their illuminating bearing on the ancient doctrine of temperaments."[4]

McDougall invites the attention of his readers to his contribution to the volume, *Physiological Action of Alcohol on Human Organism*, where in the chapter on the Nervous System he has shown reasons to believe that alcohol, chloroform and ethyl act primarily on the synaptic function of the brain blocking the brain-paths in the order from the above downward, those of the cortex being first their inhabitory influence on the lower level being thus suspended.

Goodman and Gilman have laid down the law in this respect saying:

> "Alcohol is not a stimulant but rather a primary and continuous depressant of the nerve system."[5]

Dr. Miller says:

> "Alcohol besides being absolutely avoidable as food is, when taken as something in addition to food, at all times perilous and often most harmful."[6]

4. William McDougall, *The Energies of Man*, pp. 181, 182,
5. Goodman and Gilman, *Drug and Mind*, p. 121.
6. *Alcohol. Its Place and Power*, Appendix. p. 226.

What distinguishes man from animals is that man is endowed with conscience that enables him to differentiate between right and wrong and the will-power with the help of which he chooses a right course of action and avoids the wrong one. Alcohol destroys these two remarkable qualities of man. Dr. A. C. Selmon says:

> "Almost all crimes, such as fighting, murder, rape etc., are committed while they are under the influence of alcohol. According to the record of the criminal courts, a large number of those who are punished with capital punishment have committed crime when they were under the influence of alcohol." [7]

Some of the people who are addicted to the use of liquor labour under the misconception that a small dose of liquor is not harmful. The researches conducted on the affects of alcohol on human body have established this fact beyond any shadow of doubt that liquor is harmful even if it is taken in very small quantity. With every sip of the alcoholic drink, definitely there is a loss of brain cells which is irreparable. Besides injury to the brain it does a great harm to the liver, kidney, lungs, stomach, nay, all the organs of the body. "The only real difference between the loss of brain tissues and that on the heavy drinker is one of degree."[8]

Morland says:

> "In the matter of alcoholic intake there is much leeway, for its first effect is in the diminution of self-control. In such a condition consent might well be given by a woman and with the act completed a return to normal awareness would arouse in the victim various conflicting emotions, the fears, out of these a charge of rape would come."[9]

Dr. Kinsay's work has shown that liquor (once advised as a medication for victims of heart disease to help dilate the blood vessels

7. A. C. Selmon, *Health and Longevity*, p. 103.
8. The reader's Digest, July, 1970.
9. Morland, *An Outline of Criminology*, p. 29.

that nourish heart muscles) may actually damage heart-muscle tissues by the very same capillary-clogging action it evokes in the brain. Cardiologists, therefore, no longer prescribe drinking as a means of improving circulation of blood.

Dr. A. C. Selmon, M. D., states:

"Alcohol is not a cure but it is a disease, rather a dangerous malady. Until recent years, physicians as a rule gave alcohol to the sick, thinking it would help in curing disease; but today physicians use very little alcohol as an internal medicine. It is now known that alcohol does not cure disease; on the contrary, it aggravates diseases....

"The newspapers frequently contain glowing advertisements of some brand of wine that aids digestion and energises the system. Such advertisements are gross misrepresentations. The safe rule for a sick person to follow is to avoid using any kind of intoxicating liquor. [10]

The learned author further states:

"Life Insurance Companies in all countries have found that people who use alcohol do not live as old as those who do not use it. The Life Insurance Companies state that there is twice as much sickness among alcohol drinkers as among the same number of abstainers and that there are half as many more deaths among alcohol drinkers as among the same unmber of men who do not use alcohol....

"The evil influence and harmfulness of alcohol drinking is not only manifested in the one who drinks, but it is transmitted to his offspring. In asylums for the care of feeble-minded children, it is found that 41 out of every 100 such children are the offspring of parents who drank wine."[11]

Here we quote an extract from the Report drafted by Prof.

10. Dr. A. C. Selmon, *Health and Longevity*, p. 104.

11. *Ibid.*, p. 103.

DeBore, Dean of the Faculty of Medicine and Dr. Faisans, Physician and principal, general Hospital of Paris:

"Alcoholism is chronic poisoning resulting from the habitual use of alcohol, even when this is not taken in amounts sufficient to produce drunkenness.

"It is an error to state that alcohol is necessary for workmen who are engaged in arduous manual labour, that it gives energy for work, or that it renews strength. The artificial excitement which it produces quickly gives place to nervous depression and weakness; in truth, alcohol is useful to nobody; it is harmful to all.

"The habit of drinking leads to neglect of family, to forgetfulness of all social duties, to distaste for work, to want, theft and crime. It leads, at the very least, to the Hospital-for - alcoholism causes a great variety of diseases, many of them most deadly: paralysis, insanity, disorders of the stomach and of the liver, dropsy; it is one of the most frequent causes of consumption. Finally, it complicates and renders more serious every acute illness; a typhoid fever, pneumonia, erysipelas, which would be mild in a sober individual, will rapidly kill the alcoholic.

"The hygienic faults of parents are visited upon their children: if the latter survive the first few months of life, they are thereatened with idiocy or epilepsy, or still worse, are a little later on carried off by tuberculous meningitis or consumption.

"Alcoholism is one of the most frightful scourges, whether it be regarded from the point of view of the health of the individual, of the existence of the family, or of the future of the country."[12]

This moral degeneration due to drinking of wine and other intoxicants has assumed the most fearful shade in European countries. Here is an extract from a book entitled *U.S.A. Confidential*, is quoted:

"Experts employed by the public health service secretly estimate

12. Horsley and Sturge, *Alcohol and the Human Body*.

at least 300,000 school-age narcotics addicts in the country. That's the number they know of, who have been arrested, observed, reported or who have taken treatment. The total may be a million. It takes from one to five years for a user to become an addict, so there are no statistics on undisclosed juvenile or other users." ...."The eventual purpose is not to get their few pennies when they become addicted, but to force them into prostitution and crime to support their addiction. It costs from $ 200 to $ 500 a week to keep up with a heroin habit and up to $ 1,000 a week for cocaine. Once a victim is really hooked, the money must be raised, regardless of the consequences. Boys become killers, burglars, stick-up men, dope pushers or anything; girls are turned over for prostitution, blackmail or extortion."

The Time (N. Y., U.S.A.) of 22nd April, 1975, states that after heart disease and cancer, alcoholism is the country's biggest health problem. Most deaths, attributed to alcoholism, are caused by rhosis of the liver. An alcoholic's span of life is shortened by ten to twelve years. The magazine adds:

> "In half of all murders in the U.S.A. either the killer or the victim or both have been drinking. A fourth of all suicides are found to have significant amount of alcohol in their blood streams. People who use alcohol are seven times more likely to be separated and divorced than the general population. The dollar cost of alcohol may be as much as 15 billion a year, At least half of each year's automobile death and half of the one million major injuries suffered in auto accidents can be traced directly to a driver or pedestrian "under the influence of drink."

Dr. Tony Smith says in an article in *London Times* of August, 1975, that each year 10,000 cases of alcoholism are admitted to Hospital and that alcohol is responsible for enormous amount of social destructive behaviour.

In short, it is 1400 years after the Holy Qur'an expressed its verdict about wine that the world has recognised the truth of the verdict. It has now been scientifically established that the harms of wine are greater than its benefits. The new scientific research conclusively prove that the teachings of the Holy Qur'an are pre-eminently superior to the teachings of all other religions, so much so, that in order to realise the truth of certain of its teachings which it gives in direct opposition to the teachings of all other religions, the world has had to carry on its research work for 1,400 years and has at last, after stumbling thousand times came to the conclusion that the Holy Qur'an is perfectly justified in proclaiming its verdict about wine.

CHAPTER 7

Smoking is also Injurious to Health

So far as the use of tobacco[1] is concerned, it may not be as seriously forbidden as the wine but its use is devidedly a vice, and a Muslim should avoid it as far as possible. We reproduce below English rendering of an extract from the famous book of Shaikh Yusuf al-Qardawi entitled *al-Halal wa'l Haram*:

> "The general rule of the *Shari'ah* is that it is not permissible for a Muslim to use anything in the form of food or drink which endangers his life — the process of his precipitating to death may be quick or slow. A Muslim is not the master of his being... His life, health and wealth are bestowed upon him by Allah, so it is not permissible for him to do anything which may harm him."[2]

The Holy Qur'an says:

وَلاَ تُلْقُوا بِاَيْدِيْكُمْ اِلَى التَّهْلُكَةِ ج

"And let not your own hands throw you into destruction." (2:195)

It is in the light of these observations that one can say that smoking is prohibited especially in case of a person who has been warned by a physician (of its serious effects upon his health). One thing is, however, clear about it that smoking involves sheer waste

---

1. The Red Indians of America used to snuff the smoke of tobacco through Persian Pipe having three sides like the letter (Y). They called this Persian Pipe Tobacco and from that the word tobacco was derived.
2. Shaikh Yusuf al-Qardawi, *al-Halal wa'l Haram*, p. 69.

of wealth and there lies no good in it, whether of the world or of the Hereafter. Allah's Apostle (peace and blessings of Allah be upon him) has forbidden the squandering of wealth."[3]

Modern researches have clearly shown that smoking benumbs the brain and nerves. When a man is tired or worried, he smokes and at once feels much rested. The facts are that he really does not feel better but rather he does not feel at all, because the tobacco has benumbed his brain and nerves, so he no longer feels the pain and discomfort of tiredness or worry.[4]

Smoking brings about a number of chest diseases. Tobacco causes a very poisonous substance called nicotine which is highly detrimental to human health. It causes cancer of lungs, qualm of veins, palpitation of heart, eye diseases, weakness of organs of respiration, tuberculosis, weakness of brain, cough, rheum, weakness of memory, ulcer of stomach, sexual weakness and various skin diseases.

Tobacco also contains another poisonous substance that is found in cigarettes and is called cidicianidric which is not less harmful than the former poisonous substance. Tobacco, weather it is used in the from of smoke or snuff or taken for nicotine, causes one and the same result—all the harms mentioned above. The smoker kills himself, directly or indirectly, gradually by means of the poisons that he snuffs for hours together, and which he ejects into his blood-veins, heart, lungs and brain.

Fact of the matter is that there is nothing despicable like the use of tobacco which is in use in the entire world. Particularly the whole world is addicted to smoking despite having the knowledge of its harms and extravagance that it involves.

3. *Ibid.*

4. Dr. A. C. Selmon, *Health and Longevity*, p. 106.

We seek refuge in Allah against the blind pursuit of covetousness and obeisance of Satan, the Devil.

It should be borne in mind that every game that brings about profit without anything paid in exchange, which involves usurpation of people's wealth without any justification, is unlawful like gambling with all its kinds: *cartesa jouer*, lottery etc. Similarly every activity which entails the loss of wealth and usurpation of the property of people without any legal authority, is unlawful. Devouring the property of people by lame pretexts and foul means also comes within the purview of unlawful pursuits.

We seek refuge in Allah against the accursed Satan.

CHAPTER 8

The Alcoholic's Problems

Living with an alcoholic is to tread on thorns. It is difficult for an alcoholic to maintain a normal pattern of life. The life which many alcoholics, who persist in drinking, lead is often a "fate worse than death." It is a life devoid of real happiness.

1. The Role of Alcohol in Sexual Relationship

Among other things, excessive drinking frequently relaxes the customary self-control exercised in matters pertaining to sex. Alcohol frequently removes the barriers which normally check one's inclination to over-indulgence in sex. It brings about aberrations in sex.

In the words of Dr. Ruth Fox, Medical Director of the *National Council on Alcoholism*: "The incidence of homosexuality, philandering and impotence among alcoholics is much higher than the general population. Their divorce rate is four times higher."

Alcohol affects the whole spectrum of sex relations, in the physical as well as in the emotional sense. Drinking disturbances are very frequently entwined with sexual disturbances. One reinforces the other. When Doctors or Counsellers help the alcoholic discover the basic cause of his drinking, they often find it rooted in sexual inadequacies.

In many instances a husband's drinking is tiggered by a lack of sexual compatibility with his wife. As he drinks more, the relationship deteriorates further. She becomes disgusted with his sloppiness. She may pity him, but she cannot respond to him.

He feels guilty. But rather than facing his inability, he accuses her of unfaithfulness. She may be driven to extramartial affairs. She may be pious and guard her chastity but the alcoholic husband suspects her. He becomes inimical and hostile. This results in greater impotency that drives him to more drinking. The cycle is vicious and endless.

The man who turns to alcohol for a solution to his problems is often fixed in the preadolescent stage of sex gratification. He may be a dependent personality and may have married a woman who could support his contribution to the sexual problems. But the alcoholic cannot tolerate frustration. Such characteristics make for poor sexual performance. The resulting loss of self-esteem is assuaged by drinking.

A female too may have sexual troubles at the root ofher drinking problem. She may have started drinking in order to lose her fear of men or to feel more relaxed. She may need a drink to be less sexual inhibited so as to attract men. she too lacks in self-esteem and in a mature ability to relate to the other sex.

In extreme cases such type of man or woman, besides trying to solve sexual identity problems through drinking, may try to eseape them through homosexuality or perversion.

2. The Alcoholic's Family Problems

Alcoholism can and does contribute to juvenile delinquency, divorce and anxiety. Family troubles complicate the problems of the alcoholic, such as:

1. *Economic*: As a rule, the father is the breadwinner. If he is an alcoholic, he may lose his job and jeopardize the security of his

family. When the wife is an alcoholic, she will contribute no care for the maintenance of her home. She would spend food-money for alcohol and lose interest in her appearance. She would be an embarrassment to her husband.

2. *Social Life*: Non-alcoholic partners face grim situations at times. They become increasingly reluctant to entertain in their homes or to accept invitations abroad. The non-participation of these individuals and their alcoholic mates, could create an unpleasant situation. In the end they would isolate themselves, or have the company of heavy drinkers. So, the problem worsens.

3. *Children*: It is difficult for the non-alcoholic parents to be both mother and father. If the husband is the alcoholic, the wife must find a way to earn a living. Earning a living may be easier for a non-alcoholic father, but he will encounter all sorts of problems to run the house. For example, his children may be reluctant to bring their friends home because they know "Mother is there and would not like their presence in the home." As they grow older they may become resentful. They will deliberately stay out very late. Children who come from a home where there is an alcoholic parent, often react so strongly to alcohol that they become rigid in their disapproval of it. When they become adults in their own homes, this rigidity is evidenced by not drinking, serving, buying or permitting their children to drink. This attitude may set the stage for another generation of alcoholics. On the other hand, they may imitate and adopt the alcoholic parent's method of coping with tension, anxiety and the problems of living.

CHAPTER 9

The Islamic Law and the Alcoholics

Punishment

During the time of the Holy Prophet(peace and blessings of Allah be upon him) there was no fixed punishment for an alcoholic. The accused, who was arrested and brought for trial, was beaten with shoes, kicked, given blows and thrashed with sticks and ropes. Forty stripes were the maximum punishment given for this crime.

'Abdur Rahman b. al-Azhar (Allah be pleased with him) said: I can still picture myself looking at Allah's Messenger (peace and blessings of Allah be upon him) when a man who had drunk wine was brought before him and he told the people to beat him. Some struck him with sandals, some with sticks and some with *mitakahs*. Ibn Wahb said this means green palm fronds. Then Allah's Messenger (peace and blessings of Allah be upon him) took some dust from the ground and threw it on his face. *(Abu Dawud)*

Abu Huraira (Allah be pleased with him) said: When a man who had drunk wine was brought to Allah's Messenger (peace and blessings of Allah be upon him) he told us to beat him, and some struck him with their sandals. *(Abu- Dawud)*

The Holy Prophet (peace and blessings of Allah be upon him) did not prescribe any definite punishments in different circumstances.

'Umair b. Sa'id an-Nakh'ai told that he heard 'Ali b. Abu Talib say, "If I impose *Hadd* on any one, and he (in course of punishment) dies, I would not mind except in case of drunkard. If he dies, I would pay indemnity for him because the Messenger of Allah (peace and blessings of Allah be upon him) has laid down no rule for it.

(Bukhari and Muslim)

Anas b. Malik (Allah be pleased with him) reported that a person who had drunk wine was brought to Allah's Apostle (peace and blessings of Allah be upon him). He gave him a beating with palm branches and sandals. Hadrat Anas said that forty stripes were the maximum punishment for that crime during the caliphate of Hadrat Abu Bakr (Allah be pleased with him). But when he saw that the crime was on the increase, he consulted other Companions. Hadrat 'Abdur Rahman b. 'Auf (Allah be pleased with him) said: "The maximum punishment for this crime is eighty stripes." So Hadrat Abu Bakr (Allah be pleased with him) laid down eighty stripes for this crime and Hadrat 'Umar (Allah be pleased with him) also ordered this punishment for alcoholics during his caliphate.

(Agreed upon)

Imam Malik and Imam Abu Hanifa and, according to a tradition, Imam Shafi'i, were of the same opinion. But Imam Ahmad bin Hanbal and, according to another tradition, Imam Shafi'i were of the opinion that forty stripes should be inflicted for the crime of drinking.

Thaur b. Zaid ad-Dailami told that 'Umar (Allah be pleased with him) sought counsel about the prescribed punishment for drinking wine and 'Ali (Allah be pleased with him) said to him, "I think you should give the person who drinks it, eighty lashes, for, when he drinks he becomes intoxicated, when he is intoxicated he raves, and when he raves he makes up lies." So 'Umar (Allah be pleased with him) inflicted eighty lashes as the punishment prescribed for drinking wine. *(Malik)*

Shah Waliullah has given a very thought-provoking explanation for prescribing forty or eighty lashes for drinking. He says that the best one can expect from a drunkard is that, under the influence of intoxication, he would talk nonsense and bring people into disrepute and sling mud at them. This offence falls under the category of baseless slandering the prescribed punishment for which is eighty stripes. So forty stripes is a reasonable punishment just for drinking. But with the passage of time when the people become immoderate, this punishment was enhanced to eighty stripes equal to punishment for baseless slandering.[1]

The punishment of a free person, for drinking wine or other intoxicating liquor, is eighty stripes, on the authority of all the Companions; and those eighty stripes are to be inflicted in every respect under the same rules and restrictions as in the case of whoredom.

If the drinker of wine be a slave, male or female, the punishment for wine drinking is forty stripes only, because the state of bondage induces only half punishment.

According to the *Shari'ah*, it is the duty of the Islamic State to enforce prohibition. That is why during the time of Hadrat 'Umar (Allah be pleased with him), the shop of a man, named Ruvaished, who belonged to the clan of Bani Thaqif, was burnt by his order, because wine was secretly extracted and sold there.

Pre-requisites of punishment

The following are the pre-requisites before a drunkard is punished:

1. *Sanity* : An insane person will not be subjected to punisnment for drinking wine; but a person of unsound reason will be punished.

1. Shah Waliullah, *Hujjatulah-il-Baligha*, Vol. II, pp. 164, 165.

2. *Majority* : A child will not be punished, for drinking wine for he is not held accountable for his deeds.

3. *Discretion* : A person who drinks under compulsion will not be punished, for compulsion exonerates him from sin as expounded in the following Verse:

اِلاَّمَنْ اُكْرِهَ وَقَلْبُهٗ مُطْمَئِنٌّ بِالْاِيْمَانِ

"Save him who is forced thereto and whose heart is still content with Faith." (16:106)

The Holy Prophet(peace and blessings of Allah be upon him) said:

رُفِعَ عَنْ اُمَّتِى اَلْخَطَاُ وَالنِّسْيَانُ وَمَا اسْتُكْرِهُوْاعَلَيْهِ

"My *Ummah* is exonerated of an inadvertent failure and forgetfulness and sins they are coerced to commit."

The term compulsion (*ikrah*) circumscribes the acute need of subduing indignation, the wine that sticks to the throat of a person who does not find anything to save his life and the parching thirst menacing death. Under these compelling circumstances, it is permissible for a straitened person to drink only so much wine as is sufficient to quench his thirst as Allah, the Exalted says:

اِلاَّ مَا اضْطُرِرْتُمْ اِلَيْهِ ط

"....Unless ye are compelled thereto." (6:119;2:173;5:3)

4. A man must know that the thing he eats is an intoxicant. Thus if a person drinks wine without knowing that it is wine, he will be exonerated from the sin and punishment will not be imposed on him. Similarly, if there is difference of opinion among the jurists whether a thing is an intoxicant or not, the punishment will not be imposed on a person consuming that thing because

this difference of opinion provides enough room for doubts and doubts guarantee relaxation in punishment.[2]

Mode of Evidence

Wine-drinking is proved on the testimony of two witnesses; and also by confession once made. It is seconded from Abu Yusuf, that two confessions are requisite. But it is to be observed that the evidence of woman against men is not admissible in wine drinking, because the evidence of female is liable to variation, and they may also be suspected of absence of mind, or forgetfulness.

If a person makes confession to the drinking of wine, or another intoxicating liquor, and afterwards retracts from such confession, punishment is not to be inflicted upon him, as the punishment of wine drinking is purely a right of Allah.

If a Muslim drinks wine and he is seized whilst his breath yet smells of the wine, or he is brought before the *Qadi* whilst he is yet intoxicated therewith and witnesses give evidence that "he has drunk wine", punishment for drinking wine is to be infiicted upon him; and in the same manner, punishment incurred by him when he makes confession of having drunk wine, whilst his breath yet retains the smell, because the offence of wine drinking is proved upon him and *Takadim*, or distance of time, does not appear, since the flavour of the wine still remains. This doctrine is originally founded upon a precept of the Holy Prophet (peace and blessings of Allah be upon him), "Whoever drinks of wine, let him suffer correction by scourging, as often as he drinks thereof."

If a man makes confession of having drunk wine, after the smell has ceased, in this case punishment is not to be inflicted. Imam Muhammad, however, maintains that it is to be inflicted. The same

2. Punishment will not be imposed on a person while he is in a state of intoxication and a patient will be punished after he is recovered from illness.

difference of opinion obtains in a case where witnesses bear evidence against a man that "he has drunk wine" after the smell has ceased. The reason of this diversity of opinion is that *Takadim*, or lapse of time, forbids the reception of evidence in a case of wine drinking, according to all doctors, but Imam Muhammad fixed the limitation of *Takadim*, in wine drinking, to a certain time, namely, one month (according to the most approved authorities), he conceiving an analogy between this, and a case of whoredom, because delay is established by lapse of time, and not by the ceasing of a smell. The existence or non-existence of a smell carries no weight, as there are other things the flavour of which resembles that of wine. According to the two Elders, on the contrary, *Takadim* is established by the non-existence or departure of the smell, for two reasons: First, a decree of 'Abdullah ibn Mas'ud, who, when certain persons brought before him by a man charged with drinking wine, directed that "they should examine his breath, and that if any flavour of wine was discovered, punishment should then be inflicted upon him." Secondly, the existence of the effect (namely the smell), is an irrefutable proof of wine having been lately drunk. And so to what Imam Muhammad advances, that "there are other things the flavour of which resembles that of wine", it may be replied that the difference between the smell of wine, and other articles, may be easily distinguished by one who is possessed of judgment and discernment, nor can any but ignorant persons be doubtful concerning it. Thus, according to Imam Muhammad, confession of wine drinking is not rendered ineffectual by distance of time, in the like manner as (according to him) confession of whoredom is not rendered ineffectual by distance of time, agreeably to what was before advanced, with the two Elders, on the contrary, punishment for wine drinking is not to be inflicted but on the condition that the smell still remain because Ibn Mas'ud stipulated that condition, as before stated.

If a witness seizes a drinker of wine at a time when he is

intoxicated, orwhilst he still retains the smell of the liquor, and carry him to city where there is a *Qadi*, and in the meantime the flavour or the intoxication ceases, before they arrive a the seat of justice, yet in this case punishment for wine drinking is to be inflicted upon that person, according to all the jurists, because there is an excuse for the delay, analogous to that which is created by distance of place in a charge of whoredom; and the witnesses are not suspected where such excuse exists.

If the smell of wine be discovered upon a person, or he should vomit wine yet if witnesses have not actually seen him drinking it, punishment is not incurred, because the smell alone leads but to a very uncertain conclusion, as this appearance may proceed either from the person having drunk wine, or from his having sat among wine drinkers, from whom he may have contracted the smell; and it is also possible that wine may have been administered to him by force or menaces, in which case no punishment is incurred.

Punishment for wine drinking is not incurred due to intoxication alone, unless it be known that the person has been intoxicated by the voluntary drinking of wine because men are sometimes inebriated by the use of articles which are permitted such as mare's milk; and men may by sometimes compelled to drink wine, which is not a punishable offence, when thus committed by compulsion.

The degree of intoxication which occasions punishment amounts to this, — that the person so intoxicated be not able to distinguish what is said to him in any shape; nor to know a man from a woman. The complier of the *Hidaya* observes that this is the doctrine of Imam Abu Hanifa. The two disciples have said that the degree of drunkenness which induces punishment is sufficiently found in the intoxicated person speaking confusedly and indistinctly, as it is from this that drunkenness is generally understood. Many jurists agree with the two disciples on this point. The argument of Imam Abu Hanifa is that the drinking of wine is among the causes of punishment, wherefore it is to be noticed only in the excess; for in acts which are causes of punishment the excess of them only is regarded, on account of seeking a pretext for the purpose of averting punishment; and excess of drunkenness appears in the intoxication so far overpowering the reason as not to leave the person a capacity of distinguishing one object from another (in ascertaining the illegality of intoxication produced by drinking any liquor other than wine, regards it had to what the two disciples maintain concerning the punishment for drunkenness produced by wine drinking). Imam Shafi'i, in the punishment for drunkenness, has regard to the appearance of the effect produced by the wine, in the intoxicated person's walking, or other actions, by his staggering or turning giddy when he attempts to walk: but our Doctors say that such effect may proceed from different causes, as they sometimes do not attend drunkenness, and sometimes occur in other cases (such as weakness) wherefore this species of effect is not regarded.

If a person, during a fit of intoxication, should make confession of anything which occasions punishment (such as whoredom), no punishment is to be inflicted upon him, as in such a confession, there is apprehension of falsehood, and this apprehension is to be regarded so far as to avert punishment, since punishment (*Hadd*) is purely a right of Allah. It is otherwise, however, in punishment for slander; for if a man in a state of intoxication were to make confession of slander, punishment for slander must be decreed upon him, because this is not purely a right of Allah, but a right of the individual too, and therefore, a state of drunkenness is here the same as a state of sobriety, for the sake of inflicting penalty, in the same manner as in all other matters, such as divorce, manumission, and so forth.

If a man, during intoxication, should apostatise from the Faith, his wife is not thereby divorced from him because infidelity depends upon what may be a person's belief, and that cannot be ascertained during drunkenness.

Mode of Execution

The punishment of a free person, for drinking wine or other intoxicating liquor, is eighty stripes (and to a salve forty stripes) and those eighty stripes are to be inflicted in every respect under the same rules and restrictions as in the case of fornication. The wine drinker must be striped naked to receive the punishment.

How and in what manner the punishment of flogging is to be awarded has been made clear in Islam. We give below some of its details:

1. The punishment must be administered with a stick which has no knots upon it; and that the stripes must be applied in moderation, that is to say, neither with severity nor yet with too much leniency. Hadrat Ali (Allah be pleased with him), when he was about to inflict punishment, used to smooth off from the rod any knots which might happen to be upon it, as too much severity on the one hand tends to destruction, and on the other hand too much leniency is inadequate to the design of punishment. The stripe of flog should, therefore, be neither too heavy or hard nor too tender or delicate. It should be just average both in weight and roughness. And when punishment is to be inflicted on any person, it is necessary that he be striped naked; That is to say, that all the clothes be taken off, except the girdle because the punishment in this way is administered with the greatest effect.

2. It is requisite that the eighty stripes (and in the case of salve forty stripes) be given not all upon the same part or member (limb) of the person upon whom punishment is inflicted, but upon different parts, as it might otherwise be attended with

danger to life; and none of the stripes must be inflicted on the face, the head or the privities. The Holy Prophet (peace and blessings of Allah be upon him) once said to the executioner: "In inflicting the punishment, take care not to strike the Face, the Head, or the Privities."

3. The Holy Qur'an uses the word *Jald* for flogging which is derived from *Jild* (the skin). The jurists have therefore, stated that flogging should be such as does not inflict wounds on the body beneath the skin.

4. The executioner should strike neither with full force nor so lightly as not to do any serious harm to the offender.

5. The flogging should be avoided at the times of intense heat or extreme cold. One should be flogged in the sunshine during the winter season and in shade during the hot hours of the summer season.

6. It is not proper to flog on bare back after having tied the offender to the stake.

7. It is permissible to distribute the flogging on some days keeping in view the physical condition of the criminal, but it is preferable to award punishment at one time.

8. Flogging should not be done by a cruel executioner but by scholars who are well versed in the Islamic Law so that they should award punishment according to the letter and spirit of the Law.

CHAPTER 10

Al-Maisir (Gambling)

Definition

Maisir means a game of haphazard in all matters — particularly a game of chance by means of divinatory arrows. *Maisir* is of various categories. Some of these of *Maisir* are seeking omen or fortune by divinatory arrows, back gammons, chess, lottery etc.

The word *Maisir* (game of chance) is derived from the root:

(i) *Yasara* (يَسَرَ) To become gentle, to draw lots by arrows; or

(ii) *Yasar* (يَسَار) : Affluence because *Maisir* brings about profit;or

(iii) *Yusr* (يُسْر) Convenience; ease: *Maisir* is so termed because it is a means of earning without toil and exertion; or

(iv) *Yasr* (يَسْر) : Dividing a thing into a number of shares and distributing them among themselves. Gambling is called *Maisir* because those who partake in the games of chance divide the meat of sacrificial animal among themselves.

All the above connotations are vividly found in the word *Maisir*. Imam Malik (Allah be pleased with him) says that gambling is of two categories: a game of chance that is partaken in with a view of sport (fun) and the game of chance which involves gambling. Gambling means all dealings in which people are required to make a bet and every dealing which involves some aspect of gambling is *Maisir*.

The Holy Qur'an on the Prohibition of Gambling

يَسْئَلُونَكَ عَنِ الْخَمْرِ وَالْمَيْسِرِ ط قُلْ فِيهِمَا اِثْمٌ كَبِيرٌ وَّمَنَافِعُ
لِلنَّاسِ وَاِثْمُهُمَا اَكْبَرُ مِنْ نَّفْعِهِمَا ط

"They ask thee (O' Prophet) about *Khamr* (intoxicants) and games of chance (gambling). Say: In both of them there is great harm althought there is some advantage as well in them for men, but their harm is much greater then their advantages." (2:219)

يَا اَيُّهَا الَّذِيْنَ اٰمَنُوا اِنَّمَا الْخَمْرُ وَالْمَيْسِرُ وَالْاَنْصَابُ وَالْاَزْلَامُ
رِجْسٌ مِّنْ عَمَلِ الشَّيْطَانِ فَاجْتَنِبُوهُ لَعَلَّكُمْ تُفْلِحُونَ. اِنَّمَا
يُرِيْدُ الشَّيْطَانُ اَنْ يُّوْقِعَ بَيْنَكُمُ الْعَدَاوَةَ وَالْبَغْضَاءَ فِى الْخَمْرِ
وَالْمَيْسِرِ وَيَصُدَّكُمْ عَنْ ذِكْرِ اللّٰهِ وَعَنِ الصَّلٰوةِ فَهَلْ اَنْتُمْ مُّنْتَهُوْنَ

"O' ye who believe, verily wine and games of chance, (ungodly) shrines, and divining devices are abomination of Satan's work. Avoid them, that ye may prosper. Only would Satan sow hatred and strife among you, by wine, and games of chance, and turn you aside from the remembrance of Allah, and from Prayer: will you not, therefore, abstain from them?" (5:90;91)

From these Verses of the Holy Qur'an, it is obvious that games of chance (*Maisir*) entail great sins and promises petty benefits and that *Maisir* is an abominable act of Satan. It is, therefore, imperative to avoid gambling in order to achieving success and happiness. Satan sows in our hearts the seeds of enmity and hatred against one another and turns us aside from the remembrance of Allah and His worship by means of games of chance. Its prohibition has, therefore, been declared obligatory. Similar is the case with wine. Both wine and games of chance go hand in hand to create corruption and both have been declared unlawful simultaneously.

Traditions on the Prohibition of Gambling

The Holy Prophet (peace and blessings of Allah be upon him) said: "Whosoever says to his companion: Come let us play a game of haphazard, should give alms (as an atonement)."

(Bukhari and Muslim)

It connotes that a mere invitation to gambling is such a serious sin as to warrant atonement thereof by charity. Then just imagine the position of a man who indulges in gambling. The Holy Prophet(peace and blessings of Allah be upon him) further said: "Whosoever plays back-gammon is as if he dyes his hands with the flesh of swine and its blood." *(Muslim)*

Ibn Abi Al-Dunya has reported Yahya b. Kathir as saying: "Allah's Messenger (peace and blessings of Allah be upon him) passed by people playing back-gammon. He said, "their hearts are preoccupied in sport, their hands are ill and (their) tongues make absurd utterances. Every game which involves gambling or mischief, is a game of chance (*Maisir*)."

There is no difference of opinion among the jurists that every sort of gambling is harmful, except betting for horse-race and archery which have been declared lawful for persuading horsemanship, archery and preparation for *Jihad* because Allah says:

وَأَعِدُّوا لَهُمْ مَّا اسْتَطَعْتُمْ مِنْ قُوَّةٍ وَّ مِنْ رِّبَاطِ الْخَيْلِ تُرْهِبُونَ بِهِ
عَدُوَّ اللّٰهِ وَعَدُوَّكُمْ

"Make ready for them all you can of (armed) force and of horses tethered, that thereby ye may dismay the enemy of Allah and your enemy." (8:60)

Stone-altars

As far the stone-altars, they were stones erected in and around the Holy *K'aba* in the pre-Islamic period. People used to slaughter their sacrificial animals beside these altars and seek nearness to them through worship. Such altars were 360 in number.

On the advent of Islam, these altars were removed from there. This dismantlement of altars took place on the eve of the victory of Makkah when the Holy Prophet(peace and blessings of Allah be upon him) entered Holy *K'aba* with a staff in hand and demolished them one after the other and recited this Qur'anic Verse:

وَقُلْ جَاءَ الْحَقُّ وَزَهَقَ الْبَاطِلُ ط اِنَّ الْبَاطِلَ كَانَ زَهُوْقًا .

> "And say: truth hath come and falsehood hath vanished away. Lo, falsehood is ever bound to vanish."[1] (17:81)

Every stone, clod of clay, tree or sea that is worshipped falls under the category of altars.

We, therefore, seek refuge in Allah against every wicked malignant and against the hovering Satan.

As far divining arrow (*azlam*), they are arrows cut off in thin slices of wood in the shape of arrows having no heads. In the pre-Islamic period the Arabs were taken to draw lots with a view to seeking good or bad omen.

As far abomination (*Rijs*), everything loath-some, whether physically or abstractly, is *rijs* (abomination). Accordingly, it is said *rajulun rijsun* (رَجُلٌ رِجْسٌ) i. e., an abominable man, and *rajulun arjasun* i.e., (رَجُلٌ اَرْجَاسٌ) abominable men.

---

1. These words were recited by the Prophet (peace and blessings of Allah be upon him) when he witnessed the destruction of the idols round the *K'aba* after the conquest of Makkah (Marmaduke Pickthall, *The Meaning of the Glorious Qur'an*, p. 434).

Abomination is of various kinds: abomination by nature, abomination in the eye of intellect, abomination declared as an abomination by the *Shari'ah* like wine and game of chance or an overall abomination like a corpse because it is despicable by nature and in the eye of intellect and *Shari'ah*.

Scriptures on the Unlawfulness of Gambling

As for gambling or a game of chance, the past scriptures of the Jews and the Christians i. e., the Torah and Bible have no mention of prohibition of gambling. This position is indicative of the fact that their books are not perfect and intact. It is unbelievable that the books revealed to the Prophets of Israelites would not have the provision of prohibition of gambling despite the fact that gambling entailed economic and spiritual corruption of their *ummah*.

A Brief History of the Prohibition of Gambling in Islam

The History of the unlawfulness of the games of chance *viz.*, gambling, is as old as the history of unlawfulness of wine because the prohibition of both has been declared simultaneously in *Sura al-Baqara* (2:219) *and Sura al-Ma'ida* (5:90,91) as already mentioned. But the game of chance was declared unlawful in two stages unlike wine which was declared unlawful in four or five stages.

The first stage was the revelation of Verse 2:219 in the month of Rabi-ul-Awwal, 4 A.H. (August 625 A.D.). Allah in this Verse has mentioned the game of chance (*Maisir*) as characteristic of great sin which has paltry benefits for mankind. This Verse is, therefore, a clear proof of the gradual prohibition of the game of chance.

The second and the last stage is the revelation of Verses 5:90,91 in the month of Dhi-al-Qada, 6 A.H. (March, 627 A.D.). In these Verses, Allah has totally declared gambling (*Maisir*) unlawful leaving no room for relaxation.

Nature of Gambling and the Arabs

When famine broke out the Arabs brought sacrificial animals — camels and sheep — and slaughtered them. Then they divided them into 28 shares and placed ten arrows near them, namely *fadh, tawam, raqib, hils, nafis, musbil, mu'alli manih, sanih* and *waghd*.

One out of these 28 shares one was earmarked for *fadh*, two for *tawam*, three for *raqib*, four for *hils*, five for *nafis*, six for *musbil*, seven for *mu'alli*; and *mu'alli* would receive a major share and from this a proverb came into vogue, every one who would have a lion's share of anything was called "*Sahibu al-qidhil mu'alli*. (صَاحِبَ الْقِدْحِ الْمُعَلَّى) The last three arrows *manih, sanih* and ***waghd*** had no share at all. This process always, was completed among ten persons like drawing lots.

The Arabs then distributed these shares among the needy and they themselves did not eat anything out of them. They felt proud of that act and condemend those who did not participate in this ritual. The later were nicknamed as "*baram*" i. e., a mean and niggardly men devoid of manly traits. Later on, they forgot the spirit of the ritual and made the arrows a means of business without any consideration of munifincence and help to the needy. Then a man began to gamble with all his property and as a result thereof become a destitute and penniless.

We seek refuge in Allah againt the evil promptings and deprivation of Divine Guidance.

Divining Arrows for Seeking Fortune

During the period of ignorance, the Arabs used to make ten arrows which were strips of wood without headpoints. They named them *aqlam* (pen-sticks), *qidah* (featherless arrows) and *azlam* (divinatory arrows), which were put in a *ribabah* or leather-bag tossing on the *arm*. Then a man would put his hand in it to bring out an arrow in the name of a polytheist, and so on. If an arrow having some shares was brought out for a man, he took the share specified for it and if an arrow having no share was brought out for a man he would not get anything but lose the entire cost of the sacrifice.

There were two other kinds of seeking fortune and either of them was meant for securing some information about the unseen events:

First, the keeper of the Holy *K'aba* had three arrows. On one of these was written "Do", on the second arrow was scribed "Do not do", while on the third one nothing was scribed. According to another report on one arrow was written "My Lord hath commanded me", on the second arrow was written "My Lord hath forbidden me", while the third one carried no remarks. Whenever anyone intended to go on some journey or war or wanted to marry or make a business transaction or wanted to go out for some other human needs, the custodian of *K'aba* would cast divining arrows. If an arrow having the words "My Lord hath commanded me" came out, he would go out for the job. On the other hand if an arrow with the words "My Lord hath forbidden me" was picked up, he would desist from going out. If the arrow bore no words was drawn, the same process was repeated.

The second category consisted of seven arrows. One of them was near the idol called Hubal placed inside the Holy *K'aba*. All the vicissitudes with which humanity comes across were inscribed on this arrow and the Arabs cast lots by means of it in the manner already discussed. Allah has forbidden all the three means of seeking fortune in the Verse:

حُرِّمَتْ عَلَيْكُمُ الْمَيْتَةُ وَالدَّمُ وَلَحْمُ الْخِنْزِيرِ .... اِلَى قَوْلِهِ :

وَاَنْ تَسْتَقْسِمُوا بِالْاَزْلَامِ ط ذَالِكُمْ فِسْقٌ ط

"Forbidden unto you are carrion and blood and swine-flesh"—upto the words "and that ye seek fortune by divining arrows. This is an abomination." (5:3)

Similar other Verses have also been revealed in the Holy Qur'an.

The rationale underlying the prohibition of seeking fortune by arrows is that it is an absurd and superstitious action which is followed by unwise persons. The Arabs, in this way, ascribed lie to Allah, If by "Lord" appearing in the words "My Lord hath commanded me" they meant Allah, the great and High. If by the word "Lord" they meant an idol, they were ignorants and polytheists. The act of seeking fortune by arrows leads to a claim of having the knowledge of the unseen which power exclusively vests in Allah. Again, these omens were sought by the flight of birds, divination, augury, geomancy, sorcery, magic, astronomy and also seeking fortune by beads and by all other things that deemed to have the knowledge of the unseen. All these acts are unlawful in the sight of Islamic *Shari'ah*. Allah, the Exalted, says:

قُلْ لَّايَعْلَمُ مَنْ فِى السَّمٰوٰتِ وَالْاَرْضِ الْغَيْبَ اِلَّااللّٰه ط

"Say (O'Prophet): None in the heavens and the earth knoweth the unseen save Allah." (27:65)

Again, the Holy Qur'an says وَمَا كَانَ اللّٰهُ لِيُطْلِعَكُمْ عَلَى الْغَيْبِ

"And it is not (the purpose of) Allah to let you know the unseen." (3:179)

Difference between Lots and Game of Chance

Casting of lots recognizes equal right of the persons for whom lots are drawn. Casting of lots is permissible under special circumstances when a person having an equal right and seeing that only one can avail of this right, is not going to sacrifice his right for the sake of other. Sayeda 'A'isha (Allah be pleased with her) reported that the Apostle of Allah (peace and blessings of Allah be upon him) whenever had a mind to set out on a journey, would cast lots among his wives and that wife would accompany him in whose favour fell the lots. *(Abu Dawud and Muslim)*

This procedure was adopted by the Holy Prophet(peace and blessings of Allah be upon him) because had he chosen to his own sweet will anyone of his wives, it would have injured the feelings of the other wives.

Quite contrary to this, the game of chance (gambling) does not recongise equal rights of the gamblers. Therefore, Allah has declared it unlawful and made drawing lots permissible. Allah has mentioned two events of drawing lots in the Holy Qur'an. The first event is narrated in the following Verses:

وَاِنَّ يُونُسَ لَمِنَ الْمُرْسَلِيْنَ. اِذْ اَبَقَ اِلَى الْفُلْكِ الْمَشْحُوْنِ.
فَسَاهَمَ فَكَانَ مِنَ الْمُدْحَضِيْنَ.

"Lo. Yunus (Jonah) verily was one of the (Divine) Messengers. When he fled unto the laden ship, and then they drew lots and was of those rejected." (37:139-141)

The second event is given in the following Verses:

ذٰلِكَ مِنْ اَنْبَاءِ الْغَيْبِ نُوْحِيْهِ اِلَيْكَ ط وَمَا كُنْتَ لَدَيْهِمْ اِذْ يُلْقُوْنَ اَقْلَامَهُمْ اَيُّهُمْ يَكْفُلُ مَرْيَمَ وَمَا كُنْتَ لَدَيْهِمْ اِذْ يَخْتَصِمُوْنَ.

"This is of the tidings of things hidden. We reveal it unto thee (Muhammad). Thou wast not present with them when they threw their pens (to know) which of them should be the guardian of Mary, nor wast thou Present with them when they quarrelled (thereupon)." (3:44)

In the *Torah* we have:

"Verily. by drawing lots land is distributed in accordance with the names of the descendant of their ancestors. They own according to lots and their shares are divided whether they are small or large in number. *(Chapter 27, Verses: 55, 56)*

In the sacred scriptures we come across the maxim; "Drawing lots settles the disputes and make a judgment among the strong."

(Chapter 18, Verse 8)

Verse 33 of Chapter 16 of the Holy Scripture reads as:

"Lots are cast among persons having equal rights and from the Lord is every decree thereof."

Seeking fortune by means of lots finds its mention in Verse 35 of Section 27 of Matthew as well as in Verse 24 of Section 15 of Marcurius.

It is incumbent upon all the Islamic Governments to launch a movement in their countries against gambling and its various forms just as lottery and should prescribe punishment for the defaulter. The Holy Prophet (peace and blessings of Allah be upon him) has narrated an event of the people who observe the Divine Limits (*Hudud*) and those who defy them. He (The Holy Prophet) said: "The similitude of those who establish the limits prescribed by Allah and those who infringe them is like the similitude of a people who draw lots to embark a boat. Some of them went to its lower storey and the others went to its upper storey. People staying in the lower storey, when they required water, went to those staying in the upper storey and said, "What do you think if we make a hole in our storey and do not tease those above us?" So, if they ignore them and their plans, all of them will ruin and if they hold their hands (from doing so) all of them will be fully successful." *(Bukhari)*

CHAPTER 11

Evil Effects of Gambling

Evil Effects

Gambling entails religious, social, moral and economic harms. Some of them are enumerated below:

1. Gambling distracts those who partake the game from the remembrance of Allah and Prayer. When a gambler sits continuously for hours together, he is so absorbed in it that he forgets everything around him; rather he becomes unconscious of his own, Self. He forgets his household and family. How then, can he take care of his Prayer?

2. Gambling sows the seeds of disputes and quarrels among the gamblers which ultimately assume the shape of enmity and hatred among them. This point is made clear in the following Verse:

> "Only would Satan sow hatred and strife among you, by wine, and games of chance and turn you aside from the remembrance of Allah, and from Prayer: Will you not, therefore, abstain from them?" (5:91)

3. The sin of gambling is greater than its benefit.

This Verse has enunciated two invaluable principles, namely:

(a) Dispelling mischiefs is precedent to acquiring benefits and

(b) The commission of lesser evil is obligatory when the commission of either of the two evils is necessarily essential.

4. It corrupts morals making people sluggish in waiting for providence by whimsical means and giving up activities essential for making earnings *viz*., agriculture, industry, business— the foundation stone of social living and human prosperity and happiness in this mundane life.

5. It enslaves the gambler who becomes a mute slave in the hands of gambling and seldom succeeds in abandoning it. When he earns some benefit, his greed for gambling increases and when he loses the game, even then his interest in the games of chance increases to make good the loss. In this way he remains awfully engaged in gambling till he becomes a destitute.

6. It brings about a sudden havoc in the countries due to sheer waste of wealth by losing the game.

7. It usurps the wealth of towns and transfers it to the hands of the mischief-mongers within and outside the country. thus gambling is a root-cause of innumerable economic evils reducing many rich people to destitution and ultimately forcing them to commit suicide.

We seek refuge in Allah from gambling and its ancillary sins.

Paltry Benefits of Gambling

The mundane benefits of gambling as compared with its great harms and ruinous complexities are mere whimsical benefits. If fortunately enough, you get these benefits the ultimate aftermaths thereof are unhealthy. Some of the petty benefits of gambling are enumerated below:

1. It gives some transitory pleasure to the winning gambler, for this pleasure is followed by grief as a reaction. when he suffers loss by gambling.

2. It promises munificence to the poor just as people winning

lottery, a form of gambling, build asylums and hospitals and do other good works. But the fact is that the wealth acquired by unlawful means and spent on good works have no reward because Allah is pure and He accepts only pure things. The same thing is true about gambling or lottery for it brings about a benefit to a very small group of people and causes a crushing loss to the majority of them.

3. It makes a destitute a rich man all of a sudden without any toil and in the next moment reduces a rich man to a destitute.

We seek refuge in Allah against gambling and destitution that accrues therefrom.

In short all the benefits of gambling enumerated above are imaginary and whimsical whereas its harms are real.

When the gambler spends his wealth for a fancied profit and when a person wastes his hard earned money for the fancied things having no existence, he corrupts his thinking and weakens his reason. Gambling has forced a large number of gamblers to commit suicide or made them content with living a life of humiliation and abjection.

CHAPTER 12

Emphasis on the Unlawfulness of Wine and Gambling

Firstly, Allah, the Exalted, has laid great emphasis on the unlawfulness of wine and gambling in the Verse embodying the words: "Will ye then (not) desist" (5:91). Here the imperative verb *intiha* has been used in the sense of negative interrogative form, a highly eloquent mode of expression. It is just like saying: "All the calamities entailed in wine have been recited to you and you have been warned against all its dangers; will you then, with all this information, not desist from it? Or will you follow the same path which you tread in the past as if you have not been admonished and you have not been warned against its repercussions?"

Secondly, Allah has termed it as *rijs* (an abomination) of the handiwork of Satan. Gambling has been so named that one should desist from all forms of wickedness. That is why the Holy Prophet(peace and blessings of Allah be upon him) has said about wine, "It is the root cause of all vices."

Thirdly, Allah has made a mention of wine and gambling along with the stone-altars and divining arrows which are acts of heathens and absurdities of the polytheists. That is why the Holy Prophet(peace and blessings of Allah be upon him) has said:

مُدْمِنُ الْخَمْرِ كَعَابِدِالْوَثَنِ

"An alcoholic is like a worshipper of the idol."

Ibn Maja has reported Hadrat Abu Huraira (Allah be pleased with him) as saying: "One who plays chess, indeed, disobeys Allah and His Messenger." *(Malik, Ahmad, Abu Dawud and Ibn Maja)*

Fourthly, Allah, the Exalted has declared both wine and gambling as diabolic acts because they cause corruption, injustice and invite the wrath of merciful Lord.

Fifthly, Allah has made abstention from wine and gambling as a means of success and betterment of the affairs and properties of people and eschewing wine and gambling preserves both health and security of life as well as dignity and nobility.

Sixthly, Allah has declared them a fountainhead of enmity, hatred and grudge which are most abnoxious mischiefs from which stem out most of the sins pertaining to wealth, respect and person of a man.

Seventhly, both the acts hinder people from the remembrance of Allah and from His worship which are the essence and pillars of the religion (*Din*) and which promote and perfect religion.

Eighthly, the sins entailed in them are more serious then their benefits and Allah has made the sin *haram* in th following Verse:

قُلْ اِنَّمَا حَرَّمَ رَبِّیَ الْفَوَاحِشَ مَا ظَهَرَ مِنْهَا وَمَا بَطَنَ وَالْاِثْمَ

> "Say (O' Prophet): Verily, my Lord hath forbidden indecencies, such of them as are apparent and such as are within, and sin...."
> (7:33)

The evil effects of wine and gambling, to which the humanity was not aware in the past, are now becoming manifest and testifying the fact laid down by our Lord in His words: "And the sin thereof is greater than the benefits thereof" and "it is an abomination of the handiwork of Satan." But the promptings of the baser self, the urge of self-gratification and the Satan have made the sons of Adam to indulge themselves in these unlawful pursuits and thus suffer loss of their wealth and health. The Holy Qur'an says:

وَلَقَدْ صَدَّقَ عَلَيْهِمْ اِبْلِيْسُ ظَنَّهٗ فَاتَّبَعُوْهُ

"And Satan indeed found his calculation true concerning them, for they follow him." (34:20)

لَهُمْ قُلُوْبٌ لاَّ يَفْقَهُوْنَ بِهَا وَلَهُمْ اَعْيُنٌ لاَّ يُبْصِرُوْنَ بِهَا وَلَهُمْ اٰذَانٌ لاَّ يَسْمَعُوْنَ بِهَا اُولٰٓئِكَ كَالْاَنْعَامِ بَلْ هُمْ اَضَلُّ ط اُولٰٓئِكَ هُمُ الْغٰفِلُوْنَ.

"They have hearts wherewith they understand not, and they have eyes wherewith they see not, and they have ears wherewith they hear not. These are as the cattle — nay, but they are worse! These are the unmindful." (7:179)

CHAPTER 13

Conclusion

Gleanings from the Holy Qur'an

قُلْ يَا اَيُّهَا النَّاسُ قَدْ جَاءَ كُمُ الْحَقُّ مِنْ رَّبِّكُمْ ج فَمَنِ اهْتَدٰى فَاِنَّمَا
يَهْتَدِى لِنَفْسِهٖ وَمَنْ ضَلَّ فَاِنَّمَا يَضِلُّ عَلَيْهَا وَمَا اَنَا عَلَيْكُمْ
بِوَكِيْلٍ.

"Say: O' mankind! Now hath the Truth from your Lord come unto you. So whosoever is guided, is guided only for (the good of) his soul, and whosoever erreth, erreth only against it. And I am not a warder over you." (10:108)

وَقُلِ الْحَقُّ مِنْ رَّبِّكُمْ قف فَمَنْ شَاءَ فَلْيُؤْمِنْ وَّمَنْ شَاءَ فَلْيَكْفُرْ لا
اِنَّا اَعْتَدْنَا لِلظّٰلِمِيْنَ نَارًا اَحَاطَ بِهِمْ سُرَادِقُهَا ط وَاِنْ يَّسْتَغِيْثُوْا
يُغَاثُوْا بِمَاءٍ كَالْمُهْلِ يَشْوِى الْوُجُوْهَ ط بِئْسَ الشَّرَابُ ط وَسَاءَتْ
مُرْتَفَقًا.

"Say: (It is) the truth from the Lord of you (all). Then whosoever will, let him believe, and whosoever will, let him disbelieve. Lo! We have prepared for disbelievers Fire. Its tent encloseth them. If they ask for showers, they will be showered with water like to molten brass which burneth the faces. Calamitous the drink and ill the resting-place !" (18:29)

وَيُحَذِّرُكُمُ اللّٰهُ نَفْسَهٗ ط وَاِلَى اللّٰهِ الْمَصِيْرُ.

"Allah biddeth you beware (only) of Himself. Unto Allah is the (ultimate) return." (3:28)

وَيُحَذِّرُكُمُ اللّٰهُ نَفْسَهُ ط وَاللّٰهُ رَءُوْفٌ بِالْعِبَادِ ۝

"Allah biddeth you beware of Him. And Allah is full of pity for (His) bondmen." (3:30)

وَلَقَدْ وَصَّلْنَا لَهُمُ الْقَوْلَ لَعَلَّهُمْ يَتَذَكَّرُوْنَ ۝

"And now verily We have caused the Word to reach them, That haply they may give heed." (28:51)

وَلَوْ اَنَّهُمْ فَعَلُوْا مَا يُوْعَظُوْنَ بِهِ لَكَانَ خَيْرًا لَّهُمْ وَأَشَدَّ تَثْبِيْتًا ۝

"And had they done what they were exhorted to do, it would have been better for them and more strengthening." (4:66)

رَبَّنَا لاَ تُزِغْ قُلُوْبَنَا بَعْدَ إِذْهَدَيْتَنَا وَهَبْ لَنَا مِنْ لَّدُنْكَ رَحْمَةً ج ۝
إِنَّكَ أَنْتَ الْوَهَّابُ.

"Our Lord! Cause not our hearts to stray after thou hast guided us, and bestow upon us mercy from Thy Presence. Lo! Thou, only Thou, art the Bestower." (3:8)

وَقَالُوْا سَمِعْنَا وَأَطَعْنَا غُفْرَانَكَ رَبَّنَا وَإِلَيْكَ الْمَصِيْرُ ۝

"We hear, and we obey. (Grant us) Thy forgiveness, our Lord. Unto thee is (our ultimate) return." (2:285)

سُبْحَانَ رَبِّكَ رَبِّ الْعِزَّةِ عَمَّا يَصِفُوْنَ. وَسَلَامٌ عَلَى الْمُرْسَلِيْنَ ۝
وَالْحَمْدُ لِلّٰهِ رَبِّ الْعٰلَمِيْنَ ۝

"Glorified be thy Lord, the Lord of Majesty, from that which they attribute (unto Him). And peace be unto those sent (to warn). And praise be to Allah, Lord of the Worlds." (37:180-182)

And blessings be upon Prophet Muhammad, the Apostle of Allah, and upon his progeny, and upon his Companions and on all the righteous bondsmen of Allah.

Bibliography

English Books

'Abdullah Yusuf 'Ali — The *Holy Qur'an* (English Translation).

Arthur Fisher — *Danger: Social Drinking*

Badri, M. B. — *Islam and Alcoholism*

Fazlul Karim, Maulana — *Al-Hadis* (English Translation and Commentary on *Mishkat-ul-Masabih*)

Goodman and Gilman — *Drug and Mind*

Hamilton, Charles — The *Hedaya* or a Commentary on the Musulman Laws

Horsley and Sturge — *Alcohol and the Human Body*

Hughes, T. P. — *A Dictionary of Islam*

Hussein A. Rahim and Ali Mohamed Jaffer Sheriff — *Guidance from Qur'an*

Ibn Kathir — *Tafsir al-Qur'an al-Azim*

Ibn Taimiyya — *Al-Fatawa*

Jack Lait and Lee Mortimer — *U. S. A. Confidential*

Lane — *Lexicon*

Maududi, Abul A'la, Syed — *The Meaning of the Qur'an* (English Translation and Commentary)

Miller, Dr. — *Alcohol, Its place and Power*

Morland — *An Outline of Criminology*

Muhammad Muhsin Khan, Dr. — *Sahih al-Bukhari* (English Translation)

Pickthall, Mohammad Marmaduke— *The Meaning of the Glorious Qur'an* (English Translation)

Qutb Sayyid — *Fi Zilal Al-Qur'an*

Rizvi, Saeed Akhtar, Maulana — *Inner Voice*

Robson, James — *Mishkat al-Masabih* (English Translation)

Selmon, A. C., Dr. — *Health and Longevity*

Shah Waliullah — *Hujjatullah-al-Baligha*

Siddiqi, Abdul Hameed — The Holy Qur'an (English Translation and Explanatory Notes)

— *Mishkat ul-Masabih* (English Translation and Explanatory Notes)

— *Sahih Muslim* (English Translation and Explanatory Notes)

William McDougall — *The Energies of Man*

Yusuf al-Qardawi — *Al-Halal Wa'l Haram*

Journals and Newspapers

Reader's Digest — July, 1970; July, 1976

The Time — 22nd April, 1975

London Times — August, 1975 (an Article written by Dr. Tony Smith on "Alcoholism" and published in its issue of August, 1975)

اُردو کتب ومقالات

مولانا سید ابوالاعلیٰ مودودی	تفہیم القرآن
مولانا امین احسن اصلاحی	تدبّر قرآن
مولانا سید محمد انظر شاہ کشمیری	شراب، اسلام کی نظر میں (ماہنامہ "الحق" مئی سنہ ۱۹۷۲ء)
ڈاکٹر تنزیل الرحمٰن	شراب، اسلامی مملکت کی بربادی کی ذمہ دار (ماہنامہ "الحق" مارچ سنہ ۱۹۷۲)
ڈاکٹر تنزیل ا	شراب نوشی کی سزا (ماہنامہ "الحق" جون سنہ ۱۹۷۲)
جناب ریاض الحسن	شراب وقمار (ماہنامہ ترجمان القرآن مارچ، اپریل، مئی، اگست، اکتوبر، دسمبر سنہ ۱۹۸۶ء)

عربی کتب

احمد بن علی بن حجر العسقلانی	بلوغ المرام من ادلتہ الاحکام
	یسئلونک عن الخمر و المیسر

INDEX

A

Aaron 5
'Abbas b, Maradas 22
'Abdul Muttalib 22
'Abdul Wahab 71
'Abdullah b. Husnaid 33
'Abdullah b. 'Umar 32
'Abdullah bin 'Amr 24
'Abdullah ibn Mas'ud 92
'Abdur Rahman 35, 50, 95, 97
'Abdur Rahman b. al-Azhar 87
'Abdur Rahman b. 'Auf 88
Abu Bakr 23, 40, 88
Abu Buraida 44
Abu Burda 25
Abu Darda 47
Abu Dawud 13, 24, 25, 28, 30, 31, 42, 47, 49, 87, 105, 111
Abu Dujana 44
Abu Hanifa 88, 93
Abu Huraira 13, 29, 30, 67, 87, 111
Abu Musa 25, 29
Abu Musa al-Ash'ari 29
Abu Talha 42, 44
Abu Talib 22, 87
Abu Umama 29
Abu Yusuf 91
Abyssinian 20, 55
Afringan 4
Afsus 6
Ahmad ibn Hanbal 38, 40
Ahzab 32
'A'isha 25, 28, 58, 104
Alexander Brice 73
Alyashkari 7
American 17, 63
Ansar 33, 35
Arabia 22, 55, 68
Arabic 7, 11, 24, 27, 69
Arabs 6, 7, 9, 11, 15, 19, 35, 42, 53, 54, 56, 58, 100, 102, 103, 104
'Arina 45
Armaya 6
Arthur Fisher 74
Atharva Veda 2, 3

B

al-Baqara 101
Baghdad 50
Baihaqi 33
Bani Thaqif 89
Bible 101
Bilal 55
Bolis 6, 29, 57
British 75
Bukhari 13, 18, 19, 29, 32, 42, 45, 49, 67, 88, 99, 107

C

Charle E. Ramsgate 74
Charles Richet 64
Christians 101

D

Daghdo 4
Dailamah al-Humairi 30
Dastur 4
DeBore 78

E

East 4, 9, 14, 56, 60, 61, 69, 74, 78

England 17
English 17, 18, 81
Europe 16
European 15, 64, 78

F

Faisans 78
France 64
Frederick Treves 74

G

German 63
Gilman 75
Goodman 75

H

Hakim 67
Health and Longevity 76, 77, 82
Hell 26, 31, 53, 55, 58
Hidaya 93
Hinduism 1, 4
Hodge 73
Horsley 78
Hubal 103
Hudaibiya 32

I

Ibn 'Abbas 33, 44
Ibn Abi Dunya 49
Ibn Hibban 49
Ibn Jarir 33
Ibn Kathir 38, 40, 41
Ibn Maja 15, 28, 30, 31, 49, 111
Ibn Mardawiya 33
Ibn Mundhir 33
Ibn Taimiyya 26
Ibn 'Umar 18, 19, 24, 26, 29, 40, 41
Ibn Wahb 87
Imam Malik, 97
Imam Shafi'i, 88, 94
India 2
Indian 1
Indra 1, 2, 3
Iranian 3, 4
Israelite 4

J

Jabir 26, 28
Jainism 10
Jaishan 26
Jews 31, 101
Jihad 99

K

al-Kafirun 35
K'aba 100, 103
Khadija 22
Krepelin 73

L

Lady Smith 74
Lane 18
Lexicon 18
London 79

M

al-Ma'ida 34, 35, 101
Madinah 9, 11, 34, 36, 40, 41, 44, 46, 55, 57
Makkah 34, 38, 43, 53, 55, 100
Marcurius 106
Mary 7, 75, 84, 105
Matthew 106
Miller 75
Morland 76
Mu'adh bin Jabal 25
Muqis b. Ṣababa 22
Muslim 13, 18, 19, 25, 26, 28, 31, 32, 37, 38, 42, 45, 47, 56, 57, 67, 81, 88, 91, 99, 105

N

al-Nahl 34
New York 74
Nisa'i 29

Noble 65, 66, 74
Nu'man bin Bashir 13
Nuwairi 7, 23

P

Pahlavi 4
Paradise 21, 29, 50, 53, 55
Paris 78
Persian 7, 55, 81
Pickthall Marmaduke, 69, 100
Pourushasapa 4

Q

Quraishites 33
Qur'an 11, 19, 21, 23, 27,36, 37, 38, 40, 43, 45, 48, 53, 54, 55, 56, 57, 58, 64, 67, 69, 79, 80, 81, 96, 98, 100, 104, 105, 112, 113
Qur'anic 21, 24, 32, 34, 36, 38, 40, 46, 53, 55, 56, 100
Qusayy b. Kilab 22

R

Rig Veda 1
Roman 16, 55
Ruth Fox Dr., 84

S

Salman 55
Saudi Arabia 68
Selmon 76, 77, 82
Shaiba b. Rabi'a 22
Smith Lady, 74, 79
Solomon 5
Sturge 78
Suhayb 55
Syed Sabih 72
Syria 41

T

Tariq ibn Suwaid al-ju'fi 31
Thaur b. Zaid ad-Dailami 88
Tibrani 45
Tirmidhi 15, 28, 31, 42, 49
Tony Smith Dr., 79
Torah 5, 101, 105

U

U.N.O. 64
Uhud (The battle of), 32
Umair b. Sa'id an-Nakh'ai 87
Umar b. Alwardi 60
Umar ibn al-Khattab 36
Umm Salama 25, 46
Ushah 5
Uthman 23, 49

V

Vedas 1, 2, 3
Vedic 1, 2, 3

W

Wa'il al-Hadrami 31, 47
Walid b. Mughira 22
Walker 74
Warqa b. Naufal 22
West 17, 68
West Africa 17
Western 15, 16
William McDougall 75

Y

Yahya b. Kathir 99
Yaman 25, 26
Yunus (Prophet) 105
Yusuf al-Qardawi, Shaikh, 81

Z

Zoroaster 3, 4
Zoroastrian 3, 4
Zoroastrianism 3, 4

Memo

Memo